T0163203

WALKING ON
THE COSTA BLANCA

About the Author

Terry Fletcher has been walking and climbing on the Costa Blanca for more than 30 years. He began climbing on the Yorkshire gritstone outcrops as a teenager after becoming inspired by the landmark live BBC broadcast climb on the Old Man of Hoy. He has walked, skied and climbed extensively throughout Europe and North America. He has a particular love of the sandstone deserts and canyons of the American South West.

He has been a full-time professional writer for more than 40 years, writing for almost every national newspaper as well as specialist magazines, and appearing on television and radio to comment on the outdoors. He is a former editor of *Countryman*, *Dalesman* and *Cumbria* magazines and was a senior executive at the *Yorkshire Post*. He still lives in the Yorkshire Dales.

WALKING ON
THE COSTA BLANCA

by Terry Fletcher

2 POLICE SQUARE, MILNTHORPE, CUMBRIA LA7 7PY
www.cicerone.co.uk

Route mapping by Lovell Johns www.lovelljohns.com
Contains OpenStreetMap.org data © OpenStreetMap
contributors, CC-BY-SA. NASA relief data courtesy of ESRI

Acknowledgements

Many people have helped in the creation of this book and my grateful thanks
go to, among others: Chris Craggs, whose climbing guides introduced me
to the delights to be found behind the bars and beaches, to Bob Stansfield,
whose original Cicerone guides opened up these mountains, Cherie Chapman,
Ian and Gail Craven, Dave and Sue Cobley, Geoff Hall, Harry Lambert, Jane
Spreadborough, Rod and Lynn Valentine, Keith Wright and Val Young for their
suggestions, for sharing their favourite routes with me and for their company.

To my editor, Stephanie Lambert, for spotting nonsenses.

My special thanks to Christine Kennett for her forbearance during the
fruitless toing and froing and bad language as we explored tenuous paths that
led to dead ends, impassable cliffs and impenetrable undergrowth during our
pursuit of progress.

Updates to this Guide

While every effort is made by our authors to ensure the accuracy of guidebooks
as they go to print, changes can occur during the lifetime of an edition. Any
updates that we know of for this guide will be on the Cicerone website (www.
cicerone.co.uk/751/updates), so please check before planning your trip. We
also advise that you check information about such things as transport, accommodation and shops locally. Even rights of way can be altered over time. We
are always grateful for information about any discrepancies between a guide-
book and the facts on the ground, sent by email to info@cicerone.co.uk or by
post to Cicerone, 2 Police Square, Milnthorpe LA7 7PY, United Kingdom.

Front cover: On the crest of the Serra Ferrer North Ridge (Walk 14)

CONTENTS

Symbols used on route maps

~~	route	♗ ✝	church/cross
---	alternative route	🏰	castle
≈≈	additional route	⬆	manned/unmanned refuge
Ⓢ	start point	•	water feature
Ⓕ	finish point		
ⓈⒻ	start/finish point		
ⓈⒻ	alternative start/finish point		
<<<	direction of route		
	woodland		
	urban areas		
~	main road		
—■—	station/railway		
▲	peak		
⚐	campsite		
■	building		

Relief

1400–1600
1200–1400
1000–1200
800–1000
600–800
400–600
200–400
0–200

SCALE: 1:50,000

0 kilometres 0.5   1

0 miles   0.5

Contour lines are drawn at 25m intervals and highlighted at 100m intervals.

Warning

Mountain walking can be a dangerous activity carrying a risk of personal injury or death. It should be undertaken only by those with a full understanding of the risks and with the training and experience to evaluate them. While every care and effort has been taken in the preparation of this guide, the user should be aware that conditions can be highly variable and can change quickly, materially affecting the seriousness of a mountain walk. Therefore, except for any liability that cannot be excluded by law, neither Cicerone nor the author accept liability for damage of any nature (including damage to property, personal injury or death) arising directly or indirectly from the information in this book.

To call out the Mountain Rescue, ring the international emergency number 112: this will connect you via any available network. Once connected to the emergency operator, ask for the police.

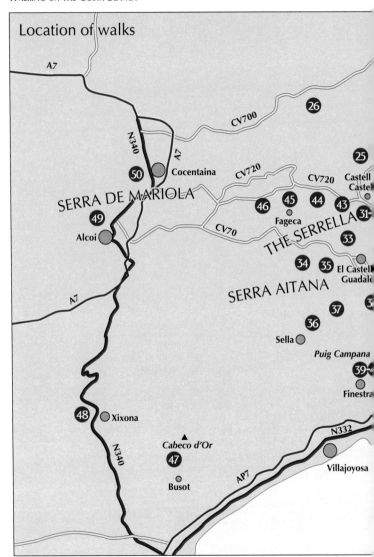

Location of walks

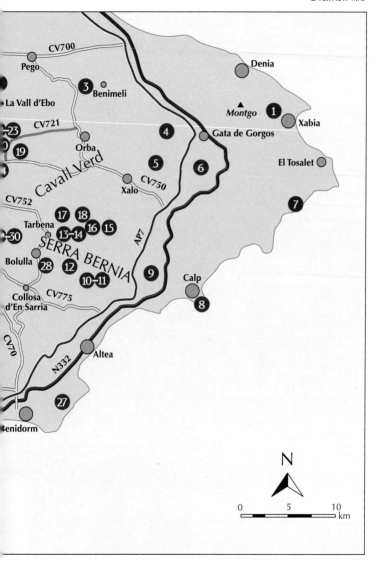

Bernia Circuit (Walk 10)

INTRODUCTION

The 'sleeping lion' of the Ponoig as seen from near Polop

Think Costa Blanca and, as likely as not, you'll think Benidorm and lager louts. Well get ready to think again.

It's true that this was one of the first areas discovered by tourists during the package holiday boom of the 1960s and 70s, helping to make Benidorm Europe's biggest holiday resort, but in recent years those who came in search of sun and sangria have been joined by a new kind of visitor not content to pack the bars and clubs into the small hours and sleep it off on the beach next day. First it was climbers who discovered the 'sun rock' potential of the inland crags and coast but in recent years they have been joined by growing numbers

of walkers and cyclists so that today rucksacks and bike bags increasingly jostle with the matching Samsonite and fake Louis Vuitton on the baggage carousels of Alicante.

The key lies in a climate that offers more than 300 days of sunshine a year. Summer temperatures may be stiflingly hot but for the rest of the year they are more amenable to exercise, akin to those of an English spring or summer.

And just beyond the beaches and high rises lies a completely different world of accessible, rocky mountains rising to 1500m – higher than Ben Nevis – and knife-edge ridges that stretch away in long chains of gleaming white limestone pinnacles like the bleached skeletons of dinosaurs' spines. Of deep, dry *barrancs* – the local catchall that encompasses everything from wild canyons winding their way for kilometres on end between the mountains to narrow gullies etched deep into the slopes – where it is possible to walk all day and not see another soul. Of slopes clothed in pine-scented forests or olive and orange groves. Of valleys dusted with the delicate pink and white blossoms of almond trees growing on miles of terraces laboriously hacked from the hillsides centuries ago by desperate farmers but which are now often being slowly reclaimed by the mountains. Of narrow paths where your boots kick up the fragrance of wild herbs leading to

still-used fonts, springs and wells that made life in this arid landscape possible. And all set against the backdrop of the glittering blue Mediterranean which adds a beguiling extra dimension to any day out.

The embryonic footpath network is often based on centuries-old trading routes dating back to the long occupation of Spain by the North African Moors, their old cobbles and steps still clear beneath your boots. Nowhere are these old ways more remarkable than on the aptly-named 10,000 Steps (Walk 22), which penetrates the formidable depths of the imposing Barranc del Infierno (Hell's Gorge). Others climb to the ruins of castles and watchtowers perched improbably on rocky spires, another legacy of the religious and ethnic wars. Today

Looking from Monte Ponoig to Castellets Ridge (Walk 39)

The path leading to the col between the North and South Ridges of the Ferrer (Walk 14)

the old trails are being supplemented by more modern paths as the local authorities begin to cater for a new type of visitor. Simultaneously active walking groups, notably the Costa Blanca Mountain Walkers made up largely of British ex-pats, are reclaiming lost trails and in some cases, quite literally, carving new ones through choking undergrowth to lost valleys and inaccessible summits. The result is an initially strange but ultimately bewitching mix of wild mountain walking cheek by jowl with modern development, especially near the coast, and all within a couple of hours' flying time from shivering Britain. Small wonder that the *serras* of the Costa Blanca have become a favourite winter adventure destination for sun-starved Brits and other

northern Europeans, many returning year after year under the spell of these magical mountains.

GEOLOGY

Even the most cursory glance will reveal that these mountains are made of limestone, creating a type of landscape that geologists and geographers call karst. It is a porous and soluble rock which explains the almost complete absence of running surface water or lakes and conversely the almost universal presence of dry ravines and gorges worn out of the underlying bedrock over millions of years.

The rock was formed 200 million years ago from the compressed remains of countless sea creatures that fell to the ocean floor. The rock moved northwards on shifting continent-sized tectonic plates and when plates collided huge areas of rock were thrust upwards, creating ridges and mountain chains with much of the present landscape shaped within the last five million years.

The Costa Blanca lies at the northern extremity of the Betic Cordilleras that stretch from Andalucía in southern Spain in an arc culminating in the islands of Ibiza and Majorca and contains sizeable areas of limestone pavement with blocky clints divided by grykes. Where the pavement is clear it can make for easy walking, as on the Alt de la Penya de Sella (Walk 36), but where the ground is covered by vegetation it becomes treacherous, providing a strong incentive to stick to the paths.

Below ground the landscape is equally dramatic with water creating underground passages and channels. More than 6000 caves have been recorded with exploration revealing more all the time. Show caverns, such as the Coves del Canelobre, passed on Walk 47, offer the non-caver a glimpse of what lies beneath.

WILDLIFE

If there is a single major disappointment to walking on the Costa Blanca it is the distinct shortage of wildlife or at least visible wildlife. Many blame this on the Spanish passion for hunting and there may well be truth in that, although whether that is because the creatures have been annihilated or merely become sensibly wary of humans is debatable. In any event the creatures you are most likely to see are wild goats and birds. Boar are relatively common but are mostly noticeable by the dug over earth they leave in their wake. They are not normally dangerous and, unless cornered or protecting young, will usually beat a swift retreat. Wild lynx, polecats and foxes are similarly shy – with the notable exception of a fox that turns up at the bar in Famorca in search of titbits. Red squirrels, now rare in the UK, may also be seen.

There are also several species of snakes, although you are more likely to see them flattened on the road than meet them in the undergrowth. Only the vipers, identifiable by zigzag markings and triangular heads, are dangerous and even their bite is rarely fatal, but should be treated swiftly. Statistically bee stings kill more people. More unpleasant too is an apparently humble caterpillar. The pine

*Famorca's
bar-crawling fox (Walk 44)*

Nest of the processionary moth...do not touch!

processionary moth takes its name from the way its caterpillars, once they leave the silky nest they spin in pine trees, move nose to tail in lines which can be two to three metres long. Do not be tempted to touch them. The hairs are extremely irritating and can cause serious allergic reactions. If one should drop on you do not brush it off with your bare hands. It is said the only solution if you get the hairs on your clothing is to burn the garment!

Birds are nowhere near as commonplace as they should be but with an estimated 70 per cent of European species either resident in Spain or passing through as migrants there are some spectacular sights to be seen. Most colourful are the hoopoe, the golden oriel and the bee-eater, while birds of prey will occasionally be spotted, including griffon vultures around the Barranc del Cint (Walk 49), eagles and peregrine. Choughs are also common in the mountains.

The coastline possesses a wealth of seabirds while just inland the salt lake of Calp is home to flamingos, egret and cormorants. The rice marches north of Denia are popular with bird-watchers, as is the Albufera Natural Park south of Valencia.

PLANTS AND FLOWERS

The area's gentle climate means there are flowers virtually all year round but February and March are generally acknowledged as providing the finest displays. Although hardly wild, the almond groves are explosions of pink and white blossom while beneath the trees are carpets of daisies. It may seem odd to get excited over a lawn weed but the sheer number of flowers makes the showing spectacular. The profusion of wild orchids can be particularly striking. With more than 3000 plant species identified in Alicante Province it is impossible to

Dwarf daffodil

name them all, but many are dwarf varieties. Dedicated botanists will be kept happy for hours while the general walker can simply enjoy the uplifting effects of the mid-winter displays of colour as rising paths climb through vertical zones from lush Mediterranean to Alpine.

HISTORY

The story of the Costa Blanca is etched into its landscape, the names of its villages and the faces of its inhabitants. The earliest evidence of Man is to be found in the cave paintings of Petracos, near Castell de Castells, passed on Walk 25, which are thought to date back more than 5000 years. Later came Phoenician and Greek traders to be followed by the warring armies of Rome and Carthage as they fought to control the Iberian Peninsula. The Carthaginians founded Alicante but ultimately were no match for Rome.

However, the most significant invasion was by the Moors from North Africa crossing the Straits of Gibraltar in 711. Within five years they had reached Alicante and began a rule that lasted 600 years. During that time Christians were tolerated and allowed to practise their religion. These Mozarabs were largely responsible for creating a remarkable network of trading routes across the mountains. They were so well-engineered that many still exist today and form some of the most popular walks, notably the 10,000 Steps (Walk 22). The Moors, with their knowledge of

Mozarabic trail 10,000 Steps (Walk 22)

Fort de Bernia (Walk 10)

irrigation and water handling, were also instrumental in establishing for the network of wells and fonts still in use today.

A much more visible legacy of centuries of war is the huge number of *castells*, which sometimes seem to crown almost every hilltop. In truth most are little more than watchtowers but exploring these mountains you will find no shortage of Penyas del Castellet. Since the name means Castle Hill this is hardly surprising since, if there are two things here in abundance, they are castles and hills.

After centuries of Moorish rule came the Reconquista (Reconquest) in the 12th century when Alicante was again brought under Christian rule. Some Moors, who converted to Christianity, were allowed to remain and it was not until 1609 that they

were finally expelled from the region, though coastal raids by Berber pirates continued long after. The events are still celebrated in lavish annual festivals of Moors and Christians, mostly between August and October, re-enacting the great battles and the taking of each town.

The Arab influence still remains, not least in the names of many towns and villages. Most common is the prefix Beni, meaning 'sons of' and usually refers to a tribe or clan. Other names beginning Al are also often Moorish in origin. Their other lasting imprint is in the huge number of agricultural terraces climbing high in the hills and sometimes to the very summits. Many date from the time of Moorish rule but others from a later population explosion, which demanded more ground be brought into production.

GETTING THERE

Thanks to its long-established tourism infrastructure, the Costa Blanca is perhaps the most accessible of winter destinations with regular, often daily, flights from most major UK and northern European airports to Alicante, the main gateway to the Costa Blanca. Murcia to the south entails a slightly longer drive.

Those who want to take their own vehicles face either a long drive across France or a ferry to Santander or Bilbao. The A7 motorway runs just inland from the coast but tolls can be expensive. Even the relatively short 60km stretch from Alicante to Calp costs more than €5 (2015).

Trains and buses run up the coast from Alicante to the major resorts.

GETTING AROUND

The inland villages of the Costa Blanca are not blessed with the most comprehensive public transport system and, with the exception of a bus service option for Walk 27, readers will be reliant on cars at the start and finish of each day. With this in mind, almost all of the walks have been devised as circular. Car hire is relatively cheap, sometimes as little as £30 or £40 a week in winter, and is best arranged before arriving in Spain. Most major international hire companies as well as numerous local ones have bases at Alicante airport. Be aware, however, that although most offer unlimited mileage some restrict users to 2000km

per car, after which the vehicle must be exchanged. Exceeding the limit can result in punitive charges of €2 a kilometre. New UK rules on paperless driving licences also came into force in summer 2015 (see www.gov.uk/news/driving-licence-changes).

The alternative to car hire is to stay in one of the mountain villages that offer local walking or where property owners are prepared to offer a taxi service, as many will.

See Appendix C for more public transport details.

WHEN TO GO

The length of the walking season depends on your tolerance to heat but in general late autumn to early spring is most likely to suit UK and Northern European visitors. Even the locals avoid the summer heat. September and October boast average temperatures still in the high 20s but may also be affected by the *gota fria*, a cold wind that also brings spells of rain, while December and January can provide short-lived snow, especially in the highest mountains. But generally the months from November to early April have temperatures in the high teens while still bringing an average of six or seven hours of sunshine a day. Rainfall is highest in November.

February has the added attraction of the spectacular display of almond blossom while March to May brings out the finest display of wildflowers.

Almond blossom and the Serra Bernia (Walks 10–12)

WHERE TO STAY

Accommodation is plentiful on the coast, especially in Benidorm, which has more beds that any other European resort, and countless companies offer package deals. However its boisterous 'charms' are not for everyone. Altea and Albir a little further up the coast are more sedate. Calp is a popular base for walkers. It has apartments and hotels aplenty and no shortage of restaurants and bars while still retaining a very Spanish atmosphere.

Those who prefer to stay among the mountains will find increasing numbers of *casas rurales*, self-catering villas as well as B&Bs, hotels and hostels, many catering for walkers and some offering guided walking or at least the prospect of transport to and from the hills. Popular villages include the very pretty Guadalest; Sella and Finestrat, which are convenient for Walks 36 and 37 and those around the Puig Campana; and Castell de Castells, which can be a handy base for exploring the Serrella and Aixorta (Walks 31–32 and 43–46). The string of towns and villages of the Vall de Pop (still better known to many Brits as the Jalon Valley) such as Xalo, which is well-served with bars and restaurants, and the smaller Alcalali are well placed for exploring Walks 10–18. At the top of the neighbouring Vall de Laguar are the quiet villages of Fleix and Benimaurell, which overlook the cleft of the Barranc del Infierno but are less well served either for eating or entertainment. Typing 'Costa Blanca accommodation rentals' into any search engine will bring up a wealth

Market in Sella

of choices. Those lucky enough to be able to take extended breaks can often negotiate cheaper rates.

For those on a tight budget or who prefer to be right in the heart of the mountains there are basic climbers' refuges, notably at Sella, Guadalest and Pego.

WHAT TO TAKE

Clothing

On some of the more popular mountains you may meet people wearing light trainers and even sandals but comfortable walking boots with solid soles and plenty of tread are strongly recommended. Not only will they provide ankle support and give a better grip on eroded paths they will also protect feet from the battering dished out by hours of walking on sharp limestone.

Sun-worshippers may be tempted to pull on their shorts at the first glimpse of the Costa Blanca's blue skies but before you do so remember the vegetation here is typically Mediterranean. It often consists of thorn bushes or shrubs with sharp, spiky leaves that will mean that after a week or two of walking your shredded legs may have little left to show of that hard-won suntan. If you are determined to wear shorts pack the zip-off variety that will at least give the option of covering up if the undergrowth becomes too painful.

Sun hats are essential at almost any time of the year but so too is warm clothing. Temperatures in

Wild March day on Montgo (Walk 1)

winter at high altitude can be chilly and winds strong. A sunny morning on the coast is no guarantee of similar temperatures in the mountains.

Equipment

The normal mountain gear of spare food, clothing and windproofs, plus, in winter, waterproofs as well as map, compass and a torch should be carried. Even if you do not normally use trekking poles they are worth considering. Not only will they provide a couple of extra points of contact on steep and loose paths they also come in handy for fending off the aggressive vegetation and even the occasional farm dog. The latter also usually respond to bending down as if picking up a stone. Or even to genuinely picking up a stone for that matter.

WATER

Water is often at a premium in this arid landscape and walkers should make sure they have plenty with them. Even in winter at least a litre per person is recommended and in summer much more may be needed. Old wells and springs that dot the mountains are well preserved and often clearly marked on signposts and maps.

Font del Moli (Walk 35)

21

However, although they are often still used by locals and even townsfolk who come to fill copious numbers of bottles from them, most fonts take their supply straight from the mountain. It is impossible for the casual visitor to verify their purity so without a lifetime's immunity it may be safer to carry your own supply. That said, I have from time to time made use of the springs to top up water bottles and not come to harm – yet.

SAFETY AND INSURANCE

Through necessity many of these walks have been done alone and I have occasionally been taken to task by Spanish walkers for this. It's hard to argue with them. Despite the intensive development along the coast these are lonely mountains and on many walks I did not see another person all day. On some an injured solo walker might not be discovered for days and mobile telephone cover is patchy, especially in the barrancs, so a companion is always a wise precaution.

Unlike the UK, there is no volunteer mountain rescue service and the regional government has warned that those who have to be rescued 'through negligence' will have to pay the cost of the rescue. If a helicopter is needed that could amount to thousands of euros, so visitors should be certain their holiday insurance covers them for all their planned activities and, if necessary, take out the specialist cover through organisations such as the British Mountaineering Council or the various specialist providers. See Appendix C for details.

PATHS

These walks are chosen to give a taste of everything the area has to offer, from deep ravines to high ridges and picturesque villages to rocky summits. Many make use of the constantly improving PR-CV (sometimes abbreviated to PR-V) network of Pequenos Recorridos de la Communidad Valenciana. The name means 'short walks' although some can be more than 50km long. They are 'short' only to differentiate them from the long-distance GR network. Some of the most enjoyable paths are old Mozarabic trails (see History).

The need for circular routes has meant leaving out some excellent linear expeditions only available to those with access to two cars or a driver willing to drop them off and collect them at the start and finish. That would open up a whole new range of possibilities, notably full traverses of the various *serras*. Many of the PR-CVs are based on old trading routes between towns and villages and can only be fully explored by those with these flexible transport arrangements.

The paths and tracks used vary from rural and forestry roads to narrow trods that are little more than goat trails across steep slopes. The status of a path as a PR-CV should not be taken as meaning it will be either clear or maintained. Paths generally receive little attention and can be badly eroded and loose. A useful approach is to prepare for hard pounding and to welcome the easy sections or forest trails carpeted with pine needles as a welcome bonus. Because of the aggressive undergrowth, often hiding fissures in the limestone, any path is usually safer and infinitely preferable to bushwhacking.

Despite their proximity to the holiday beaches these are serious mountains with all the hazards that entails and are neither to be underestimated nor taken lightly.

WAYMARKING

The only consistent characteristic of the waymarking is the infinite variety of ways it finds to be ingeniously inconsistent. Even on paths of the same status, such as PR-CVs, it varies from excessively lavish to near invisible. PR-CVs are marked in yellow and white, occasionally on official signposts or, more frequently, with paint flashes on rocks, walls and trees. Two straight lines mean carry straight on, curved lines indicate a turning while crossed lines mean you are going the wrong way, probably having missed a junction.

In addition some villages also have a network of local paths, *senderos locals* (SLs). Often little publicised beyond the village boundary, you may find them marked on a noticeboard in the village square or

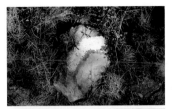

From top: Markings showing a change of direction, straight on and wrong way

a local bar may have a leaflet. The more official ones are marked with green and white paint, mimicking the PR-CVs, while more impromptu tracks tend to have occasional splodges in whatever colour was to hand.

Signposting tends increasingly, but again not always, to be in the regional tongue Valenciano rather than Spanish and sometimes even switches between languages on the same walk. In the text, a pragmatic approach has been taken of using whichever name seemed, at the time of writing, to be most helpful given local signing.

23

As everywhere, signposts are at the mercy of vandals, souvenir hunters and grumpy landowners and can appear and disappear with alarming speed. Exploring an alternative finish to one route I discovered the most useful marker post had disappeared literally overnight.

MAPS AND LANGUAGE

It is said that a man with a watch always knows the time while a man with two watches is never quite sure. Those raised on the comforting certainties of the Ordnance Survey may come to feel much the same about Spanish maps. The only series to completely cover the area are the IGN 'Military Maps', which, to put it kindly, enjoy less than universal acclaim. In recent years they have been joined by various commercial competitors such as Terra Firma, El Tossal and Discovery. These are a vast improvement but as yet none covers the entire area.

Difficulties can also arise when trying to use different maps simultaneously, a problem compounded by the use of the competing languages, Spanish and Valenciano. The latter was suppressed during the rule of General Franco but is now making a strong comeback on road signs, waymarkers and, increasingly, on maps. The reintroduction is not being prosecuted with the aggressive vigour and even venom shown further north in Catalunya but the changeover is gathering pace. Road signs and waymarkers which were once in Spanish and later bilingual are more and more exclusively in Valenciano. Brits who have long had a love affair with the Jalon Valley now find only Xalo signed from the main road and Calpe is losing its final 'e'. Benidorm remains forever Benidorm.

Mind your language... Spanish sign converted to Valenciano

The Serra Bernia (Walks 10–12)

This mix of languages throws up different spellings and occasionally even different names for the same places, which may bear little relation to each other. Readers are very strongly advised to carry the appropriate large scale map as well as the book. These can be bought from the larger suppliers in the UK and are available in Spain from shops such as the Libreria Europe in Calp, which also operates a mail order service. See Appendix C for details.

The main maps recommended are Serra Aitana, Serra Bernia, Montgo and Les Valls (Terra Firma), Costa Blanca Mountains (Discovery) and La Serrella and Serra Mariola (El Tossal).

A short Valenciano–Spanish–English glossary is given in Appendix B to help you follow maps and signs as you walk.

USING THIS GUIDE

Information is given in a box at the start of each walk description, and also listed in the Route summary table in Appendix A, to help you choose the route that's right for you.

Distances are given in kilometres and heights in metres. Because of the nature of the terrain and the quality of paths some of the walks demand a greater degree of mountaincraft and ability to navigate and move over difficult terrain than others. Please heed the warnings in the text and pick your routes accordingly.

Timings are as walked by me, a sexagenarian with high-mileage knees, and are inevitably subjective. They should be treated as a rough guide only until you have walked a few of the routes and had a chance to compare our respective paces. Please ensure adequate daylight to complete

The abrupt headland of the Serra Gelada towers over the Benidorm high rises, from Calp

the walks until you have got the measure of my timings, which do not allow for stops.

Likewise the grade of difficulty is as I personally found it. Please take note of any warnings in the text. Easy routes are fairly gentle strolls. Moderate walks demand more effort and may involve rough going. Strenuous routes are demanding days, often with steep climbs and/or descents. The scrambles are about Grade 1 but may be exposed and broadly compare to routes such as Bristly Ridge or Crib Goch in Snowdonia or Sharp Edge in the Lake District. Some entail large drops.

A fast-changing region

All the routes were walked or re-walked especially for this publication. However, the Costa Blanca is an area in constant flux. Floods, fires and landslips can wreak dramatic changes within hours while at lower levels development continues apace. The financial crisis of 2008 stalled the building boom for a while before it regained momentum, fuelled in part by money from Eastern Europe. This means that some dirt roads are gradually being metalled or concreted, while new roads, or even entire developments, will appear over time.

If you come across a problem or a change please contact me via the publisher (see 'Updates to this Guide' in the prelim pages) so that alterations can be posted on the website and incorporated into future editions.

THE NORTH

On the summit of the Tossal Grau with Montgo in the distance (Walk 2)

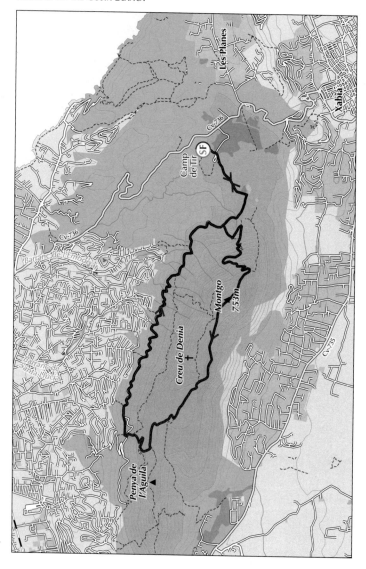

WALK 1
Traverse of Montgo

Start/finish	Plana de Justa, near Xabia
Distance	15km
Grade	Strenuous
Time	6hrs
Terrain	Rough paths, some exposed, steep ascent and descent
Height gain	800m
Map	El Montgo Parc Natural (Terra Firma)
Access	Leave Xabia on the CV 736 Denia road. After passing the 6km sign look out for the Camp de Tir les Planes Denia shooting range on the left. Some park by a barrier after 200 metres but a sign warns that vehicles may be towed away so instead carry on for another 200 metres to park by the shooting range.
Note	This is not only a tough climb, starting very close to sea level, but much of the route is on awkward terrain of blocks of limestone demanding care.

Montgo sits aloof from the rest of the Costa Blanca mountains, towering over the towns of Xabia and Denia. Its isolated position means it stands out in any view to the north, where its vast bulk looms in solitary splendour. Seen end-on from Xabia, its long ridge hidden from view, it is an intimidating pyramid throwing down a fierce challenge, demanding to be climbed. This walk accepts that head-on before enjoying a long ridge walk and an exciting descent.

▶ From the barrier at the entrance to the shooting club take the path signed 'Ruta Campo Tir – Cim 3.5km, time 2hrs'. Follow the path into the scrub heading for the mountain, which is all too obvious in front as a disconcertingly steep ridge. Where the path meets a wider dirt road turn right, still aiming for the mountain and an information board. At a three-way signpost go left following the signs for the Cim. For the next two hours or so little

No walk in this book is more comprehensively signed.

The exposed shelf path to the summit

Throughout this first section Montgo itself blocks the view inland to the mountains and the walk is very much a maritime expedition with views up and down the coast.

is required by way of navigation. Simply follow the clear and stony path as it climbs relentlessly, weaving backwards and forwards across the slope. ◄

Eventually the path turns a corner and the inland ranges come into view from Calp to the Serrella. The path crosses an exposed shelf before a final short scramble where a sign reading 'Sender Perillosa' (dangerous path) points the way to the summit with its trig column. Thanks to Montgo's solitary position the views from the summit are magnificent and uninterrupted in all directions, including along the ridge, which we now follow. The path descends to a tree and then drops again to contour the southern side of the ridge below a cross, the **Creu de Denia**, which can be visited by a diversion.

The path eventually crosses a low col and then drops to curl round a deep barranc to another col guarded by a solitary tree, where Denia comes into view. Drop down the path and traverse leftwards across the slope until you reach a junction with a path heading steeply down a gully and marked on a ground-level plaque to Denia. Take this. Initially the path is very steep and covered in loose stones. Fortunately the barranc soon becomes broader and the angle a little less precipitous as the path is able to make full use of its width. Nevertheless do not drop your guard too much; the lower section still has its moments and is exposed in places.

The path eventually comes to a T-junction. Turn left, signed 'Raco del Bou'. Just as the path seems about to tumble into the swimming pools of Denia it reaches The Cami, which is wide and partly cobbled. Here head right-wards along the broad road, as it traverses high above the coastline in marked contrast to the wild mountain walking of just a few minutes earlier. At a fork take the upper option signed 'Cova del Camell'.

After about 4km the Cami deteriorates into a narrower path and almost at the same moment the shooting club comes into view. The path continues round to the Cova del Camell where the walk has a final sting in its tail with a short, sharp ascent out of the barranc. After this the path leads across the plateau, passing an incongruous triangulation pillar, to rejoin the outward path.

WALK 2
Tossal Grau

Start/finish	Pego
Distance	11km
Grade	Moderate
Time	4hrs
Terrain	Good paths, steep descent
Height gain	773m
Map	Costa Blanca Mountains (Discovery), Les Valls (Terra Firma)
Access	It is worth avoiding Pego's intricate one-way system if possible and to approach the town via the CV 715 from the southeast. Pass the road to Vall d'Ebo on the left and shortly after take a prominent fork on the left just before a white church. Continue along this road following signs to the Calvaria. By a children's play area turn left up a wide road lined with cypress trees. Just before it crosses a riverbed turn left again following signs for Climbing.
Parking	Roadside at a fork where the tarmac runs out and becomes concreted.

Pego and Vall d'Ebo lie at the northern limit of the area that can be reached easily from the main Costa Blanca resorts and the Tossal Grau sits neatly between them, a fine limestone peak blessed with two dramatic barrancs and a network of paths from which to explore them with relative ease. This walk begins from the edge of Pego but is soon among wild mountain country and leads to an airy summit with extensive 360 degree views of the surrounding mountains and coast.

From the fork go up the concrete road to quickly reach another junction. Take the right hand branch following a sign for the PR-CV 58 to Figuereta and Xical passing

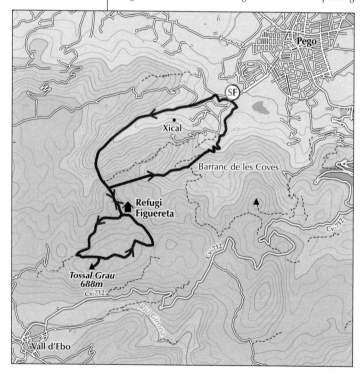

orange groves and houses. The track soon takes a right hand bend and 20 metres further on an unsigned path climbs up the banking into the undergrowth on the left to begin the ascent. When it reaches a broader unmade road carry on uphill. Ignore a junction to the right and follow the yellow and white paint flashes. After 50 metres take a track climbing off left still following the paint marks. When the path reaches another concrete road turn left.

After another 200 metres up the road turn sharply back leftwards on a footpath marked with yellow and white paint. Eventually, about 50mins from the car, the path emerges onto the rim of a plateau by some ruins and continues along a spur, following the line of a wall, with the deep Barranc de les Coves to the left. Eventually it switches sides of the ridge, now overlooking the equally impressive Barranc de la Canal while ahead masts crown the summit of the Miserat.

When the path reaches a small col, a painted arrow points off downhill. Ignore this and instead carry on leftwards up the slope to reach a signpost. Turn right to follow the signed PR-CV 58 to Figuereta. The other path, a

Looking down into the Barranc de la Canal

green and white marked sender locale goes to Pego and will be part of our return route. For now carry on uphill.

The path reaches the **Refugi Figuereta**, a fine looking building blessed with a pump and shaded picnic tables grouped around it and a good place for a rest.

Leave it, still on the PR-CV 58, now signed to Ebo, which departs from the bottom left corner of the grounds and descends towards a barranc, which it crosses and then goes onto more open slopes, squeezing between dwarf palms, until it meets a finger post at a fork with a sign pointing back to Figuereta. Here leave the PR-CV leftwards, aiming for the rocky knoll of the Tossal above.

When the path, now marked by green and white flashes, reaches a col with a marker post Montgo comes into view ahead. Here turn right to climb the final slopes to the summit of **Tossal Grau**. ◀

From the top go back down to the marker post passed just before the final climb and this time turn right, following a path which traverses the hillside across old terraces and walls. This is the continuation of the SL used earlier and it descends to pass a farm building before coming to a T-junction. Turn left, now back on the PR-CV 58 signed to Figuereta and heading back to the refuge.

From the refuge retrace your route down the ascent path, now signed to Pego, until you reach the marker post passed on the way up and here turn right along the SL signed to Pego, Barranc de les Coves.

The path crosses the slopes and begins to drop steeply down abandoned terraces before being funnelled into the barranc on a steep and loose path to pass old wells. When it finally reaches the valley floor by wooden railings go straight ahead down the unmarked track heading towards Pego. The track, which seems unlikely at first as it ploughs into the undergrowth, soon improves and takes you past the climbers' crags on the other side of the gorge before carrying on down to join a road to arrive back at the car.

The top is boulder-strewn with Vall d'Ebo below, hills all around and views to the coast and the rice-growing marshes between Pego and the Mediterranean, now also a haunt of birdwatchers

WALK 3
Serra Segaria

Start/finish	Benimeli
Distance	6km
Grade	Moderate
Time	3hrs
Terrain	Mainly on good paths
Height gain	350m
Map	Costa Blanca Mountains (Discovery)
Access	From the N332 coast road take the CV 715 through Xalo towards Pego and turn off right at Sagra on the CV 729 to Rafol and Benimeli.
Parking	On the main road below the village.

On the Costa Blanca all ridges are measured against the magnificent Bernia and inevitably tend to be found wanting. But in any other company the Segaria would be rightly lauded, a cockscomb of limestone pinnacles that catches the eye of travellers on the road to Pego. This relatively short walk climbs an old mule track to the ridge to visit some prehistoric ruins before making its way around the back of the mountain on waymarked paths to return to the start. It provides fine views out of all proportion to the scant time and effort it demands.

From the main road walk up into the village where there are two squares, the smaller being the Placa Rector Domenech. Leave this by its top right hand corner towards the ridge. Almost immediately go up a flight of steps into Carrer Calvari. From the top of the steps turn left aiming for the small Stations of the Cross, each in its small white shrine on a path marked with green and white flashes. ▶

Follow the Stations up another flight of steps and keep going until you pass between two water tanks. From the top of the Stations turn half left beside a wire fence and passing a pair over even older Stations, making your way towards a deep gully leading up to the

This whole walk follows a recently designated and improved SL, the CV-109, but in places it is also marked with the yellow and white flashes of the PR-CV network.

Station of the Cross depicting Christ's first fall is passed on the way to the first col

ridge. The path climbs steadily up the barranc to a col where it reaches two marker posts

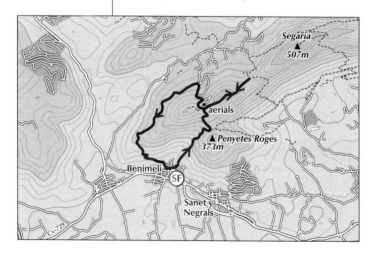

Although this **path** is now very dilapidated the remains of pitching and steps suggest it was once an important route, probably supplying a Moorish fort on the top. Just by the marker posts is a dry well and water trough where the mules, which once used the trail, were watered and rested after their climb. The post also points the way to the Poblat Iberic, the remains of a village that has been dated back to around the third century BC.

One PR-CV carries on straight ahead but another joins the SL109 in going left, as indicated by the post to weave up overgrown terraces aiming for the transmitter aerials on the ridge above. Go up this. At the ridge the path encounters a tarmac road and a picnic area with stone benches and tables, which provide a handy spot for a welcome rest. The path continues up the road to squeeze between the buildings of the transmitter station and **aerials** and then carries on along the ridge, first on the north side and then the south with the double summit of the Segaria ahead.

Summit towers of the Serra Segaria above the prehistoric Iberian ruins

The **views** have opened up in all directions. To the
north the coastal plain and rice-growing marshes
stretch away while to the east Montgo is seen from
a particularly impressive angle and to the south the
ridges of the Cavall Verd and the Bernia stand out
from a crowd of peaks. The Segaria itself is revealed
as a broad crest stretching away to a pair of huge
rocky towers.

The paths comes to a belvedere at the foot of the
first tower with fine views of the archaeological remains
clinging like swallows' nests to its side. From here the
route becomes a serious scramble and this is the end of
the road for walkers.

Return to the picnic area and from just below it a
path, signed with green and white flashes, heads off
downhill through the dwarf palms of the northern slope.
It plunges steeply down at first before starting to trend
generally leftwards across the slope until finally curving
right to rejoin the road. Turn left down this for five minutes to reach a house with a large concrete water tank
beside it. Just above the tank a track goes off left signed
to Benimeli.

It drops gently across the hillside and eventually
joins a farm track. Turn left along this as it curls round
the end of the ridge. About five minutes further on it
meets a concrete waterpipe and the path breaks off to
follow it downhill briefly before the green and white
flashes of the SL indicate a left turn down abandoned
terraces making for **Benimeli** and entering the village
close to the Placa Major.

WALK 4
Fonts de Pedreguer

Start/finish	Capelleta de Sant Blai, Pedreguer
Distance	12km
Grade	Moderate
Time	3hrs 30mins
Terrain	Clear paths and exemplary waymarking
Height gain	550m
Map	Costa Blanca Mountains (Discovery)
Access	Leave Pedreguer on the CV 720 towards Alcalali and on the outskirts of the town double back left, following signs to the Ermita, onto the Avenida Maria Lopez, which becomes the Carrer del Migdia. Follow this to a T-junction and turn right into the Carrer Passatage.
Parking	In Carrer Passatage.

Water is precious in the dry landscape of the Costa Blanca and ancient wells and springs are still tended and marked. This gentle walk, following one of the variations of the PR-CV 53 Sender de Pedreguer, visits several of the springs emerging from the Muntanya Gran – 'the Big Mountain' – behind the town. Clear paths and consistent waymarking mean navigation is seldom a problem on this ramble through a countryside that is less demanding than among the bigger, more dramatic, hills, which feature in the distant views.

From the car park walk downhill and turn into the Carrer Meravelles and just before a left hand bend go right up a ramp to join a path which traverses above the houses. Ignore a path breaking up right and carry on to where the main path reaches a concrete track by a play area. Turn right up this to a brick path but after a few steps turn left by a wooden information board, as indicated by yellow and white paint flashes on the ground, to pass down the left hand side of a building apparently used for barbecuing to reach a path and turn right uphill following the PR-CV 53 to the Font Colberta and Font d'Aixa. ▶

Leaving the rooftops of Pedreguer behind, a much older landscape comes into view. The shape of Montgo dominates the view and beyond it Ibiza floats on the horizon.

Fiesta flags in Pedreguer

Carry on following the path up the rim of the barranc and after about 40mins it passes a ruined *casita* with a deep well and a couple of minutes later comes to a sign embedded in a large cairn announcing that Pedreguer is 1.7km behind while the Font Colberta is 800 metres ahead and Font d'Aixa another 4.1km.

As the path crosses a col the jagged tops of the Bernia and Olta emerge as well as a colourful collection of villas across the barranc. Zigzag down the terraces to reach the **Font Colberta**. ◄

The font proves to be an old arched well, still with clear water in it but a sign suggests it is not drinking water.

From the font turn up the initially concrete track to pass a house guarded by a large Buddha among the trees by its gate and immediately afterwards, at a four way junction, carry on up the hill and 100 metres later come to a sign on the left to the **Font del Rull**. A flight of restored

Font Colberta

stone steps climbs the few metres to the font, which is little more than a black iron door over the old cistern.

Continue up the hill for a little under 10mins to where it meets a dirt road on the left signed to Barranc de l'Aigua. Turn left onto this but after just a couple of dozen

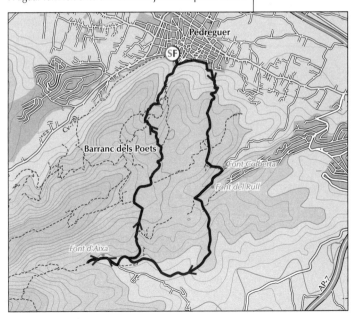

Across the barranc from the house are the Font d'Aixa climbing crags and teams are often to be seen on the routes.

paces turn right by a cairn onto a narrow path heading off downhill with the Bernia in front. It traverses round a large bowl across gentle slopes until it turns a corner and broken cliffs and sharp summits come into view with a grand, newly-built house in the valley below. Follow the path as it winds down to it. ◄

Carry on down the concrete access road of the house until, on a bend, as you pass another house on the left, a track marked with yellow and white paint goes off leftwards across the hill. Follow it until it comes to a junction and here turn sharply back right down to a road and turn right. This dogleg can be avoided by staying on the concrete road to reach the same spot but the path is more pleasant underfoot.

The road now passes houses and orange groves and a sign pointing right to Pedreguer per Aspres. This is the onward route but it is worth continuing a couple of hundred metres further to visit **Font d'Aixa**, one of the larger pools in the area. From there go back to the 'Aspres' sign and turn up the concrete track which passes a casita and quickly dwindles to a footpath. Keep climbing until it reaches a fairly long level section and about 20mins after leaving the road comes to a fork. Take the left branch, which continues to climb and traverse until after a few minutes it comes to another concrete road with a sign 'Pedreguer per Poets 3km'.

Turn up this and in less than 5mins come to a right hand bend where a sign points leftwards to Castell d'Aixa. Go up this path and where it comes to olive groves at the top of the first slope there is a T-junction of paths. Turn right, passing a tumbledown casita and following yellow and white paint as it traverses round the bowl. Ignore a path dropping leftwards.

As it continues Montgo and the colourful villas seen earlier reappear. When it reaches a junction turn right signed to Pedreguer. The town is now visible at the foot of the **Barranc dels Poets**, whose name refers to wells rather than versifiers. At a three-way junction carry on downhill to **Pedreguer** and at the next junction turn left guided by ample paint marks to arrive back in the car park.

WALK 5
Castell d'Aixa

Start/finish	Font d'Aixa
Distance	10km
Grade	Moderate
Time	3hrs 30mins to 4hrs
Terrain	Limestone paths and a high, easy ridge
Height gain	490m
Map	IGN Pedreguer
Access	Leave the N332 on the CV 750 to Xalo and after 4km take a narrow road on the right signed to Lliber. Follow it to the village where it emerges on the main road at a tricky exit where you turn right for 100 metres and then left on the CV 748 to Gata de Gorgos. After 3.8km, opposite a large white house, turn left onto the Camino Font d'Aixa, which winds between houses and on for another 2.5km to the pool of the Font.
Parking	By the font.

Little remains of the old fortress of Castell d'Aixa sitting high upon its ridge but that is no reason to shun a visit. This route follows a steep path to a col below the castle and returns via a high ridge with fine views to the coast and inland mountains, as well as over the Vall de Pop.

From the parking area by the Font d'Aixa carry on forwards following yellow and white markings. After about 100 metres look out for a turning to the left where the path begins to climb the hillside, following signs to Castell d'Aixa and Font de la Xima. At the next junction with a three way sign carry on climbing, following signs to the Castell.

The path goes up steeply until it reaches a band of rock where it climbs rightwards up a narrow shelf and passes below a fallen boulder before regaining the open hillside and soon afterwards breasts the ridge to open

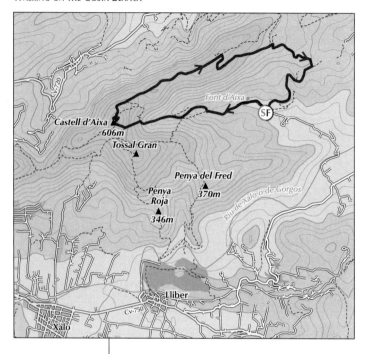

up excellent views across the valley to the castle ruins perched on the rocky summit opposite. From the col the path traverses the hillside making for another col at the head of the valley with views down into the Vall de Pop and across to a pair of dramatic shark's fin ridges on the opposite hillside below the castle. Now turn rightwards up the broken limestone slope, the route still marked with yellow and white paint flashes.

At a fork take the lower right hand option which traverses the hillside before coming back leftwards through old terraces and walls to reach the summit of **Castell d'Aixa**. ◄

Crowned with a round concrete post, the summit is an ideal place for a refreshment stop to admire the wide-ranging views.

Leaving the summit, set off along the ridge with the isolated massif of Montgo directly ahead to the northeast. After about 150 metres look out for a cairn on the edge

of the left hand slope and a path leading downwards. It initially heads back left before cutting back right aiming for the col between the summit and the next knoll on the ridge. It drops down an eroded section to a well, a surprising find at this altitude.

Castell d'Aixa rises above the orange groves

The path continues along the ridge line, by-passing subsidiary tops and passing another well before it drops down to the right with a long level section. As it drops again continue heading downwards with Montgo still ahead. At

The rock ramp climbing to the first col

a crossroads of paths continue straight across and onwards past a ruin. At the next junction ignore a path heading downhill but continue ahead along a now much narrower path still marked with yellow and white paint. At the end of the ridge a sign points the way back right to Font d'Aixa. The path now heads back up the valley through old terraces aiming for a col. It then passes through an area of renovated terraces planted with olive trees. At the end of the restored terraces continue across the hillside, ignoring a path down to the left, and still aiming for the shallow col. Cross this and continue heading down leftwards aiming for a concrete road where you turn right downhill signed to Font d'Aixa.

After about 250 metres on a left hand bend a signpost points down the road to Font d'Aixa per Barranc de Aigua. Ignore this and instead take the path which heads rightwards away from the road. This is unmarked but is in fact part of the PR-V53 and leads to Font d'Aixa via Aspres. At first it runs horizontally across old terraces into the valley, whose skyline you have just walked before, dropping steeply downhill. It passes an old casita before becoming broader and then reaching the concrete road used on the approach. Turn right along this for a 200 metres to **Font d'Aixa**.

WALK 6
Tossal del Moro and the Serrillas

Start/finish	Gata de Gorgos
Distance	12km
Grade	Moderate
Time	3 to 4hrs
Terrain	Good paths
Height gain	470m
Map	Institut Cartografica Valencia, Pedreguer
Access	Gata de Gorgos is on the main N332, 20km north of Calp. As you enter the town from the south pass under a railway viaduct and park.
Parking	Roadside bays or an unmade car park.

The hills around Gata de Gorgos are neither the highest nor the most dramatic of the Costa Blanca but that does not stop them providing very enjoyable walking. This walk begins in the gorge of the Riu Gorgos and climbs through gentle forests to a pair of summits offering excellent views and then a surprisingly wild climax as it returns to the town.

Turn towards the town and almost immediately go left over a wide bridge spanning the riverbed. On the other side turn right into a paved recreation area and drop down to the riverbed and walk to the far end, following yellow and white paint flashes which soon lead upwards into a narrow residential street. Follow this to a T-junction with a wider road. Cross straight over and go down the Carrer Penon to drop down a flight of steps to re-enter the river gorge on a developed walkway following the PR-CV

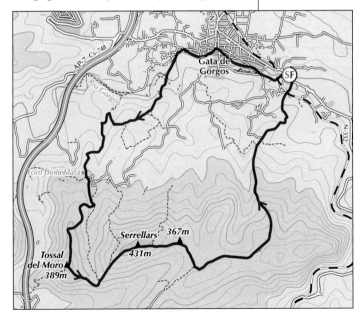

412 to Font de la Mata and Cumbre de la Serrillas. Follow this paved 'promenade' to a flight of steps leading up to a parking area overlooking the gorge. Take the road running above crags and behind houses.

The path now leaves the PR-CV and instead follows red and white flashes as it continues above the barranc. After a couple of minutes along the track, just after it has turned left downhill, look for a path cutting back on the right still marked with red and white paint heading downhill. Take this to cross the riverbed again and climb the opposite bank and at a crossroads of paths go straight ahead. After another 15mins the path reaches a fork. Carry on up the right hand branch marked by a symbol which looks like two letter 'C's back to back in red paint.

The path comes to a crossroads by a tumbledown casita. Turn right, following the red and white marks, along the broad stone-surfaced track. It passes between houses to reach a tarmac road. Turn right down this and follow it as the surface deteriorates to reach a PR-CV signpost on a junction. It is worth making the short signed detour to **Font de la Mata**. ◄

The font sits on a shelf below a small crag. It has a deep well and a small array of heavy carved stone drinking bowls once used for watering pack animals.

Towards the summit of the Tossal del Moro

At the junction turn left (or right if you visited Font de la Mata) to the Cim Serrillas and after about 5mins up the track there is a right hand bend where a path breaks off to the right marked with a pair of painted crosses. Ignore this and go round the bend to where a broad track climbs away to the right. Go up this. It weaves through terraces and passes a renovated casita, beyond which it becomes a narrow path climbing the slope to the ridge. The path then climbs leftwards up the ridge to the sharply conical summit of the **Tossal del Moro**.

On the top are the remains of a **watchtower** and a large cairn. The view takes in the Penyo Roig, Cavall Verd, Carrascal de Parcent, the Bernia, Olta and the great isolated tooth of the Penon de Ifach above Calp. Below is the rather less welcome intrusion of the Alicante–Valencia motorway. Turning your back on the road it is easy to pick out the next objective, the Serrillas, with a clear path leading down to a col and up the opposite slope.

The path drops down through pine trees to reach a ruined casita in the col before reaching a signpost to the Cim dels Serrellars. ▶

The path climbs over a subsidiary summit to the main top, which is crowned by a trig column mounted on a large plinth with extensive views. From the column do not continue along the ridge but instead head off downhill on the clear path with yellow and white markings. The path curls down and then back to rejoin the descending ridge. Then, guided by a line of substantial cairns and passing a ruined casita, after a kilometre it comes to a three way junction, here turn left signed to Gata. From here the way is clear, following paint flashes and eventually the buildings of **Gata de Gorgos** below. ▶

As the path reaches a patch of tarmac at a three-way junction carry on straight ahead, still following the yellow and white marks. When, at the bottom of the hill, it reaches a railway line turn left and then pass under a railway bridge to the **N332**. Go left to the car.

If time is pressing it is possible to make a direct return to Gata, 4km away, by carrying on down the valley following the signs.

On the way it passes a suspiciously large cairn, which on further investigation turns out to be the housing of a well.

WALK 7
Castell de Granadella

Start/finish	Cumbre del Sol, near Benitatxell
Distance	8km
Grade	Easy/Moderate
Time	3 to 4hrs
Terrain	Broad tracks for the most part but a rough section along the clifftops plus a narrow coastal path protected by chains
Height gain	350m
Access	Leave the N332 on the CV 740 for Teulada and follow signs for Benitatxell. Go through the town and at a set of traffic lights on its northern edge take the right hand fork signed to Cumbre del Sol. Go up the hill, past a mirador and into the complex, following signs for Hipica.
Parking	Roadside by the Hipica stables.

First time visitors to the Costa Blanca can be surprised, even appalled, by the scale of development along the coast and even, more recently, by the way that builders have pushed inland so that it is not unusual to find large estates of villas and apartments almost dwarfing their host villages or even sitting on sites separate from other communities. The flip side of this apparently random development is that you can sometimes use the roads of these *urbanizations* to access interesting walking and within a few minutes be in open country. One such is Cumbre del Sol, the starting point for this walk to 200m-high cliffs, an old fort and a beautiful small cove. The development borders an area set aside by the authorities in Xabia as a reserve. It is the lowest walk in the book and makes a useful option to rescue a day when the inland hills are shrouded in cloud.

Walk into the entrance of the Parc Forestal de Granadella along a broad track. Even though a backward glance shows villas climbing the hillside, the view ahead of woods and a deep barranc is entirely natural. Stay on the broad track as it clings to the rim of the barranc, following yellow and white markers and ignoring all tracks to the right. After the track swings rightwards pass through a chained entrance. At the next junction is a three way sign; take the right hand option marked PR-CV 354 Cala Granadella por Castell.

When the road briefly becomes concreted carry on, passing a large water cistern, and on along the now unmade track to a signpost. Go right still signed to Cala Granadella and Castell on the PR-CV 354. Tall cliffs now stretch away rightwards and the path arrives at the **Mirador de Llevant**. ▶

After the mirador the wide track becomes a narrow path heading downhill making for a rocky promontory just ahead. The path, still liberally marked with yellow and white flashes, clambers over miniature rock steps and squirms between sea holly and dwarf palms to the headland. From there it is possible to see down into the bay as the path drops towards sea level. Go down following marker posts until at the bottom of the slope the path reaches the ruins of **Castell de Granadella**.

It is a bit early for a prolonged stop but this viewpoint deserves a few minutes to admire the rock architecture.

This horseshoe-shaped **redoubt** was part of a chain of defences built in the 18th century to protect the area against North African pirates and was intended to deny them a safe landing spot in the cove. It had a cannon and small garrison but they certainly meant business with walls 3 metres thick. It was,

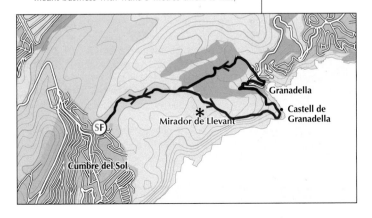

Castell ruins and cove

however, destroyed in an attack by the British during the Napoleonic Wars.

The cove, worthy of exploration, has brilliantly turquoise water making it a popular spot for divers and snorklers. During the holiday season there is a bar and restaurant.

From the ruins climb back up a few metres to the descent path and take a narrow track heading rightwards towards the cove. It climbs slightly and has one polished short descent and another narrow section soon afterwards equipped with chains. Once past these obstacles it climbs a flight of steps to pass behind a line of villas where it reaches a concrete road. Go steeply down this. At the bottom a signpost shows the return path. ◄

From the bottom of the concrete road a signpost points up the PR-CV 354 Variante Teuleria and Variante Gorugu up the Cami de la Teuleria. The road passes between villas and quickly becomes unmade. At a junction carry straight on up the left fork, quickly entering the dry bed of a barranc. Within a few minutes the PR-CV splits with the Variante Gorugu continuing up the bed while the Teuleria heads off left climbing steeply up the slope, signed to Granadella. Take this. At the top of the initial climb it passes a ruin before emerging on a spur where a well-engineered path completes the ascent.

As it nears the top the bulk of Montgo appears to the right while ahead the less impressive collection of Cumbre del Sol also come into view. When you reach a signpost passed on the way out carry on straight ahead, signed 'Mirador de Granadella' to reach the concreted stretch of road and retrace your steps to the car.

INLAND FROM CALP

Serra Bernia rises above the almond blossom (Walk 10)

WALK 8
Penon de Ifach

Start/finish	Calp
Distance	3km
Grade	Moderate
Time	2hrs
Terrain	Limestone paths, slippery in places, and some easy scrambling
Height gain	332m
Access	Entering Calp follow signs for the Port and Penon de Ifach. Park in the car park of the Parc Natural de Penon de Ifach.
Note	Some visitors bring torches for the short tunnel section but most will find the light filtering in from either end sufficient. Beyond the tunnel the character of the walk changes. The paved path gives way to polished limestone and dirt tracks, occasionally exposed but the trickiest sections and brief stretches of scrambling are equipped with rope handrails.

The Penon de Ifach is no lonely mountain. It is the giant 332m-high molar that separates Calp's two beaches. As the most prominent feature of almost any coastal view of the Costa Blanca it throws down an unavoidable challenge to all walkers and provides an easily accessible goal for a short day. But do not expect to have it yourself. Tourists by the thousand make the climb. It is also a place of Easter pilgrimage and renowned locally as the traditional cure for New Year hangovers.

Go through the gates and follow a paved path up past the information centre, through the turnstiles and carry on climbing with wide views down the coast to the Puig Campana and the Serra Gelada. As the path reaches the foot of the cliffs it enters a tunnel carved through the rock. As this is such a popular route the floor is polished to a marble-like smoothness but rope handrails ease the passage.

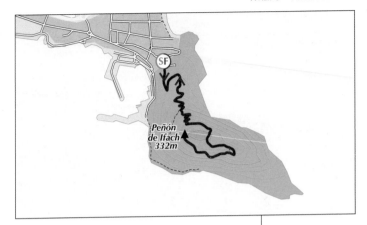

After the tunnel the path takes a long, almost level, diversion towards the seaward end of the Penon. At a junction take the path that climbs back rightwards signed to the Cima.

Penon de Ifach

The **summit** provides tremendous views up and down the coast taking in Montgo in the north and southwards to the Serra Gelada, Benidorm and beyond as well as the giants of the inland mountains. More surprising is the discovery of a colony of feral cats, which eke out a living catching birds and cadging snacks from visitors.

After savouring the views and perhaps throwing the moggies a few titbits descend by retracing your steps The care needed on the polished limestone means the descent will take almost as long as the climb.

If you have time to spare it is also worth following the **paved promenade**, which leaves the yacht club and curls round the foot of the Penon. It goes out to the end of the headland giving excellent views of Olta (Walk 9) across the bay as well as the massive cliffs on the seaward side of the monolith.

WALK 9
Serra de Olta

Start/finish	Zona d'Acampada, Calp
Distance	9km
Grade	Moderate
Time	3hrs
Terrain	Forest tracks, narrow paths and a short scramble
Height gain	440m
Map	Institut Cartografica Valencia, Calp
Access	Coming from the north on the N332 take the exit Calp Sur, from the south take the Calp Sur exit, go down to the first roundabout and double back on yourself to go under the main road follow signs to the estacion. Go past the station and then cross the tracks and drive 2.5kms uphill following signs to the Zona d'Acampada.
Parking	Official car park.

Olta is Calp's own mountain and although this walk starts on the town's doorstep it takes in a fine summit and some rugged country as it circumnavigates the massif and visits its 587m summit for a magnificent panorama of the coast and inland mountains. This is a classic example of Costa Blanca coastal walking, crossing rough country but with tower blocks below.

Leave the car park at its rear through a pair of stone gates and immediately take a path on the left signed 'PR-CV 340', which will be followed throughout the route. When the path reaches a forest road turn left. At a junction carry on leftwards following signs for the Ermita Vella. At the next fork take the uphill option still following the PR-CV 340.

At the **Ermita Vella**, a popular picnic spot, the road curls uphill, signed the Cim d'Olta. At the next junction a couple of hundred metres further on continue following the Cim d'Olta. After another 100 metres take a narrow

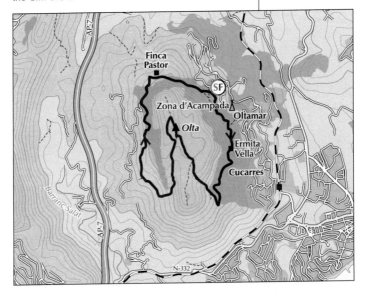

The Olta massif from Calpe

path uphill. Now the hard work begins as it follows the bed of gully and, while never overly taxing, a degree of agility will prove useful.

Where the path levels out it meets a signpost which offers a brief diversion to the subsidiary summit of La Mola but the main path presses on still following the PR-CV 340. It crosses an area of broken limestone pavement guided by yellow and white-topped posts, always heading in the general direction of a rocky saddle ahead. By a ruin turn right uphill. At the col a signpost points the way to the Cim d'Olta 300 metres away, while directly ahead the Bernia Ridge draws the eye.

A rough cairn marks what appears to be the highest point but a signpost a little further away lures walkers on. There is a rough path to it but otherwise it is a precarious boulder hop across the fragmented pavement. The sign declares this to be the summit of **Olta** although there seems little to choose between this and the cairn. Just beyond it is a dramatic drop into an impressive gully.

Having admired the view return to the col and turn right following the PR-CV 340 to the Pou de la Mola. Where the path meets a horizontal track at the top of the terraces go left to quickly reach the ruin of Corralet then head rightwards still following signs to Pou de la Mola.

This delightful section heads gently down through pines and then into a gully. At a fork take the right hand track marked Circuit Principal. After another steep descent it reaches the forest road, which is followed rightwards. This is the start of an undulating circuit of the rest of the mountain, revealing a procession of ever-changing views, firstly inland and eventually out to the coast.

At a junction turn back sharply right uphill, always following the PR-CV 340. It passes the ruined **Finca Pastor** before crossing the Pas de la Canal, which at 400m marks the last of the climbing.

The path drops down the other side becoming increasingly narrow and steep as it passes through terraces and woods with impressive crags above, a final flourish of wild grandeur before the tower blocks of Calp appear ahead.

The path eventually meets a wider road. Turn right following signs to the Zona d'Acampada. After a couple of hundred metres at a bend, turn rightwards into the trees still following the PR-CV 340. At a fork in the track take the left hand branch downhill to a signpost on the outward leg to retrace your steps to the car park.

Ruins of the Finca Pastor

WALK 10
Circuit of the Serra Bernia

Start/finish	Casas de Runar
Alternative start/finish	Casas de Bernia
Distance	14km
Grade	Strenuous
Time	4 to 5hrs
Terrain	Mountain tracks, scree – and a bit of potholing
Height gain	480m
Map	Serra de Bernia (Terra Firma)/Costa Blanca Mountains (Discovery)
Access	For Casas de Runar leave the N332 on the CV 755 signed to Callosa d'En Sarria. Pass through Altea Vella and 1km after leaving the town turn right on a very narrow road signed to Fort de Bernia. Where it meets another road slightly less than 1km further on go right and continue up the narrow road heading for the ridge. When you reach Casas de Runar a sign points right for the parking. Ignore this and carry on a short way to a level parking area. For Casas de Bernia leave the N332 at the CV 750 Xalo turn off and after 100 metres turn left to Pinos. Pass the village and at a T-junction some 14km from the N332 turn left and park just beyond the restaurants by an information board.

On any journey along the coast the Bernia Ridge draws the eye, vying with the vast monolith of the far higher Puig Campana for attention. From almost any direction it resembles the spine of a petrified dinosaur, a long chain of cols and spiky pinnacles. This walk never crests the ridge itself but instead circumnavigates the mountain before passing through the very innards of the beast by a natural rock tunnel through the crest offering a rare mountaineering experience.

The walk, described here from Casas de Runar, can be tackled in either direction and can be started from either side. Those staying in

Benidorm may opt for the southern approach from Casas de Runar, an isolated community reached via an adventurous 5km potholed road, while those staying to the north or with more respect for their car may prefer to start from Casas de Bernia.

From the houses carry on up the road bearing rightwards to a stone-clad water tank to where the tarmac ends then continue along the clear path heading towards the coast. This soon rises to the **Font del Runar**, a well protected by a steel door. From this the path, the PR-CV 7, climbs sharp left. At a scree slope the path comes to a T-junction with a path traversing the hill. Both are signed as the PR-CV 7 and we take the left hand option to the fort a kilometre away. The other direction will be our return route.

The track rises steadily across the hillside with the rock faces of the Bernia above and the three giants of

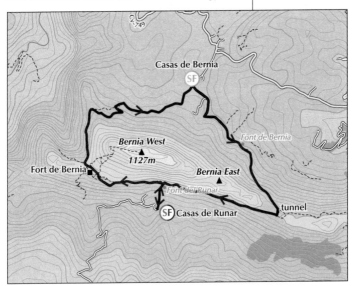

Serra Bernia

The fort would have been quite extensive with formidable defences, a dry moat and a garrison of more than 50 men.

the Puig, the Ponoig and Xanchet dominating the view to the left. The path soon reaches the remains of the **Fort de Bernia**. ◀

After investigating the ruins leave the fort still heading west beneath the escarpment making for the col ahead with the rocky towers of the Pena Severino to its left. As you reach it the onward path is revealed below heading around the end of the ridge and making for another col (see the opening photograph of this guide). This level section is easy walking with ample opportunities to admire the dramatic rock scenery and superlative distant views, including the ridge of the Serra del Ferrer running away northwards.

The path swings round the end of the ridge and becomes broader with the view changing yet again to include the isolated massif of Montgo. The easiest walking of the day now follows as the road curls down to the houses and restaurant of **Casas de Bernia**. ◀ At the tarmacked road turn right still following the PR-CV 7 now signed 'Forat' (tunnel) with extensive views to the coast and the crags of Olta in front.

This is an alternative start/finish point of the walk.

After a little over a kilometre the road reaches the rather grand **Font de Bernia** where the path climbs a flight of steps and takes to the hillside, climbing rightwards. After a couple of minutes at a fork in the path left still climbing diagonally up the slope aiming for the end of the ridge. When it reaches the rock face continue beneath the escarpment following the path past caves and notice boards but only the occasional yellow and white or blue waymarks and then up a steep limestone slab polished by the passage of thousands of feet. ▶ Finally it arrives at the tiny entrance to the tunnel and disappears into the rock.

Take particular care on this section, especially in winter when this shady side of the ridge may be iced.

At this end the **tunnel** is only a metre or so high and it is necessary to at best stoop and at worst crawl to negotiate the initial section. A degree of flexibility comes in useful for the next few metres, which feel like genuine caving and no place for the claustrophobic. The far end of the tunnel is much higher and the effort is rewarded with fine views to the mountains to the south framed in its mouth.

The path now heads rightwards along the foot of the cliffs and is suddenly profusely marked with yellow and white paint after the uncertainties of the ascent to the tunnel. It winds downwards through a field of massive boulders and then on to a scree slope, followed a few minutes

Entering the natural tunnel through the ridge

If you started from Casas de Bernia carry on ahead making for the fort and pick up the route description from there.

later by a second broader fan. Immediately beyond it you come to the three way signpost passed on the ascent from Casas de Runar. ◄ Turn left downhill signed to the Font and back to the car.

WALK 11
Bernia East Summit

Start/finish	By the junction of the CV 749 and Cami de les Cases de Verdiola
Distance	9km
Grade	Moderate/Scramble
Time	5hrs
Terrain	Forestry road and narrow ridge
Height gain	670m
Map	Serra de Bernia Marina Alta (Terra Firma)/Costa Blanca Mountains (Discovery)
Access	From the N332 north of Calp, turn off on the CV 750 towards Xalo and almost immediately turn left on the CV 749 to Pinos. Follow the road past Pinos and the Pinos restaurant. After another 3.6km take the Cami de les Cases de Verdiola on the left. Immediately after turning, park by a fork in the road.
Parking	Roadside.
Note	The ascent of the ridge involves some exposed scrambling and should be avoided in windy or wet conditions. Some may welcome a confidence rope for the most exposed sections and if in doubt be prepared to turn back.

Any visit to the crest of the Serra Bernia is an adventure to be savoured. The full traverse demands rock climbing skills and ropes but the two summits, East and West, can be visited separately by competent scramblers. The East Summit (also known as Penyes de Portixol) offers a sharp ridge, spectacular rock scenery and outstanding views along the coast and down into the Mascarat Gorge, which marks the natural end of the ridge.

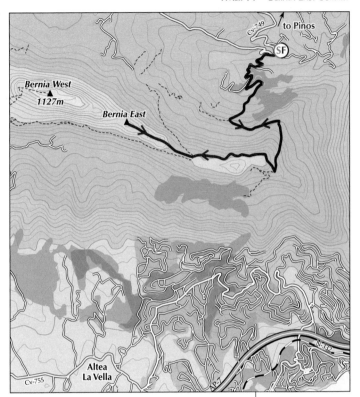

From the parking area take the right fork heading downhill into the valley. It becomes briefly unmade before the tarmac resumes, passing a *casa rurale*. Ignore a track going up to the right by a Parking Privado sign and carry on along the main track. It becomes unmade again and 300 metres later reaches a fork where there is parking for three or four cars for those who do not like the idea of an uphill walk at the end of the day. Take the left hand branch heading slightly downhill but directly towards the east summit of the ridge. Carry on following the road, ignoring a chained junction to the left until it passes a series of four houses, none of which seem to be permanently occupied. After the last one the path climbs more steeply until the track swings leftwards to run parallel to the ridge.

> Directly above, just below the **ridge**, it is possible to pick out a natural rock arch and a smaller window. Both are most easily found by following a scree scar running down directly below them, east of the main East Summit. As the path climbs it passes through the Microreserva de Flora of the Ombria de Bernia with excellent views of the ridge above. Away to the north you look down into the Pinos Valley and along the Cau Ridge (Walk 15) while Montgo dominates the distant view with the sea beyond.

Carry on up the track until, as it nears the top of the hill, it passes a small rock buttress on the right and turns a right hand bend. A few paces beyond by the first large tree a very discreet pair of cairns mark the beginning of a narrow path climbing steeply up the slope. Go up this. As you climb Olta comes into view out towards the coast and then the Penon peeps over its shoulder. The path zigzags up the slope to arrive on the ridge on a col marked by a small iron cross. Beyond, the Puig, Ponoig and Xanchet come into view, as well as Benidorm and the Serra Gelada. From here turn right to follow a faint cairned path up the rocks. As it climbs the path makes increasing demands on the hands as well as feet as it clambers over limestone flakes on the north side of the ridge. Where it drops down a rock step from a subsidiary summit to a col there is one tricky bit of route finding in the descent. The path seems to go straight ahead to reach cairns in the col below but there is a slightly easier, albeit more exposed, variation down to the right (facing along the ridge). ◄

Just above the col you pass the rock window seen from the lower slopes. To view the rock arch below, scramble down from the col itself and traverse towards it.

The path now climbs up a loose scree-covered slope to the south of a rock tower. From the top of the slope arrows and dots in faded red paint guide the way up a groove by a pinnacle followed by an easy rock staircase.

Take careful note of this for your descent as the paint marks are not immediately apparent from above. From here it is an easy scramble to the summit of **Bernia East**. A pair of bolts and an abseil chain mark the end of the fun for walkers. From here on the naked, slender rock ridge, curving away enticingly to the double summit of Bernia West, is the province of rock climbers equipped with ropes, although the West summit itself can be reached by scramblers and walkers by joining the ridge beyond the major difficulties (see Walk 12).

Descend by retracing the outward route. The crucial landmarks are the pinnacle by the paint marks, the tricky scramble and the col with the iron cross, which marks the point where the path leaves the ridge for the valley.

Natural window in the East Ridge

WALK 12
Bernia West Summit

Start/finish	Casas de Bernia
Distance	8km
Grade	Moderate/Scramble
Time	5hrs
Terrain	Steep ascent and descent, exposed scrambling and a narrow ridge partly protected by chains
Height gain	510m
Map	Serra de Bernia (Terra Firma)/Costa Blanca Mountains (Discovery)
Access	Leave the N332 at the CV 750 Xalo turn off and after 100 metres turn left to Pinos. Pass the village and at a T-junction some 14km from the N332 turn left and park just beyond the restaurants by an information board.
Parking	Roadside.
Note	Although the exertion involved is only moderate, this route entails some of the most demanding scrambling in this book. While never technically desperate, and the hardest passages are protected by chains and knotted ropes, it includes exposed sections above intimidating drops where a fall would be serious. If uncertain take a confidence rope and be prepared to turn back.

The Serra Bernia is magnet for the eye from anywhere it is visible, either seen from the side as a long serrated knife-edge ridge or end-on, apparently as a single towering peak. A traverse of the entire ridge is a full-scale mountaineering expedition requiring the use of climbing equipment. Both ends, however, can be visited by competent scramblers seeking an exciting day out. This visit to the western summit, at 1127m the higher of the two extremities, is in many people's opinion one of the best expeditions on the Costa Blanca.

From Casas de Bernia turn left along the PR-CV 7, signed 'Forat' (tunnel). Follow the metalled road for a little over 5mins until at a sharp left hand bend a narrow dirt path climbs into the trees. This trail, marked with red paint spots, climbs steeply aiming for the obvious dip in the ridge guarded by a prominent rock tower. When the track reaches the open scree slope below the ridge it divides into a multitude of options with cairns in every direction. Carry on following the red dots (or occasionally green paint) but always making for the col to the right of the prominent tower, where views open up to the Puig Campana and its neighbours.

The col, reached in an hour or so from the car, is an intimidating spot with tall rockfaces to either side. Our path lies to the right where it leads to the foot of a steep gully and the first section of scrambling. The gully is tall but never excessively difficult. At the top of the gully make an exposed step rightwards onto an area of slabs where the red spots show the way, which proves not quite as intimidating as it may appear from the gap.

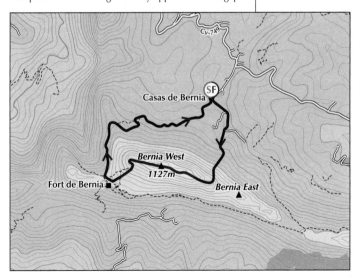

Approaching the West Summit (Christine Kennett)

After passing a subsidiary top and just before starting the climb to the two western summits the path nips from the south side of the ridge to the north to take a shelf just below the ridgeline using a path protected by a safety chain. From the top of this it is easy to see the route curving away to the summit crowned by its trig pillar. To reach the final top the path drops into a shallow notch, which is left by a chockstone-filled groove with a knotted climbing rope for assistance. From there it is just a few paces to the summit of **Bernia West** and the remains of an old watchtower.

The **setting** could hardly be bettered for standing guard with views stretching from the Algar Valley round past the Serra Ferrer, Montgo, down the length of the Bernia itself with the Penon beyond, down the coast to the Serra Gelada, Benidorm, and inland to the giants of the range, the Puig, Ponoig, Xanchet and Aitana while in the valley below the scale of horticulture can be appreciated simply by looking at the vast areas of netting over the fruit groves around Callosa d'En Sarria. From the summit it is also possible to see the wide track heading down to the Fort de Bernia below, our exit route.

The route, still following the ridge and marked by red paint, carries on down the sharp arête, descending a groove assisted by another knotted rope and crossing a smooth traverse safeguarded by a chain before crossing a very exposed shelf above a large drop, perhaps one of the most unnerving sections of the whole ridge but this time with no safety rope.

A few minutes beyond the chained section look out for a cairn marked with red paint and surrounded by a

Fixed chain on the descent from the West Summit

profusion of painted arrows and dots. The path works its way down the slope still marked with arrows and cairns but is easily lost at this point. If in doubt remember that you are heading for the fort and need to reach the broad shallow gully to the left from which the path emerges. Follow the path down the **Fort de Bernia**. ◄

The fort would have been quite extensive with formidable defences, a dry moat and a garrison of more than 50 men.

Leave the fort still heading west beneath the escarpment and making for the col ahead with the rocky towers of the Pena Severino to its left. This is part of the classic circuit of the Bernia (Walk 10). As you reach the col the onward path is revealed below heading around the end of the ridge and making for another col. This level section is easy walking with ample opportunities to admire the dramatic rock scenery and superlative distant views, including the ridge of the Serra Ferrer running away northwards.

Bulls are occasionally grazed in this area and should you happen to meet them it is advisable to give them a wide berth.

The path swings round the end of the ridge and becomes broader. The single track now becomes a broad dirt road giving a final easy section back to **Casa de Bernia**. ◄

WALK 13
Serra Ferrer South Ridge

Start/finish	El Masserof, near Xalo
Distance	6km
Grade	Moderate
Time	4hrs plus any time spent exploring the ridge
Terrain	Steep track and ridge paths, exposed in places
Height gain	400m
Map	Serra de Bernia (Terra Firma)/Costa Blanca Mountains (Discovery)
Access	From Xalo take the CV 749 signed to Bernia for 5.5km to El Masserof.
Parking	Roadside parking in the hamlet or just beyond it.

The Serra Ferrer, a great up-tilted blade of a mountain that cannot be ignored and demands to be climbed. It is divided in the middle by a twisting barranc climbing up from El Masserof. To the north (Walk 14) it is more dramatic and demanding and is the province of the scrambler. The southern part of the ridge is much broader and in places quite overgrown and lacking a good path but that is nothing that a bit more traffic and a sharp saw could not put right. Although it lacks the sheer adventure of its northern sibling it is a wonderful perch from which to survey the surrounding mountains with all the major tops seen at their very best. The Ferrer is very much a range of two halves. Standing by the roadside at Masserof it appears to be a simple, if steep, slope, cultivated in its lower sections but a mass of scrub and rock higher up. The view from here gives little hint of the drama hiding beyond the ridge with cliffs that plunge vertically into void beyond.

With your back to the Verd i Vent take the dirt road by the black and white warning chevrons that runs uphill just to the north (right) of the Casa Susi Restaurant. The road is unmarked as it leaves the tarmac but a couple of minutes up the track a mountain biking sign 'Solo experts' points off rightwards. Ignore this and carry on up the rough and stony road. As it climbs it rapidly deteriorates, becoming narrower and rutted as it gains height and slowly

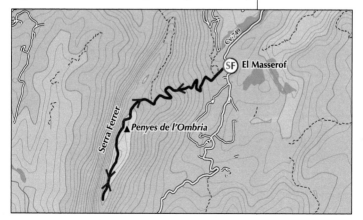

Along the way the path bypasses a couple of old wells on the right with a brace of discarded bath tub drinking troughs.

dwindles into a narrow footpath almost blocked in places by fallen trees and rocks. Soon the serrated ridge of the Bernia comes into sight with Masserof directly below as the path heads into a shallow ravine. ◄

After an hour or so of steady climbing the path reaches a col with wonderful views of the whole length of the Bernia and the Pinos valley and back past Olta and the Penon at Calp and, to the north, the bulk of Montgo. This col marks the boundary between the north and south sections of the ridge. The path crosses the col and drops a few metres down the other side before trending rightwards and then back left aiming for the **Penyes de l'Ombria**. As it continues the path slips over to the western side of the escarpment and the Ferrer shows its other face, huge cliffs, dropping down into the valley, beyond which are the peaks of the Penya Mulero, Aitana with its aerials and the distant Serrella while nearer to hand is the Carrescal de Parcent crowned with its fire watchtower.

The path crosses the head of a steep, narrow gully and climbs a muddy scree slope to emerge on the very crest of the ridge surrounded by rock with the Puig, Ponoig and Xanchet now having joined the roll call of

Serra Ferrer South Ridge

peaks along the southwestern horizon. Continue along the crest making for the 899m summit and a 360 degree panorama. ▶

It used to be possible to make a circuit from the summit by crossing the eastern slopes using a path that traversed along terraces. In recent years this has become badly overgrown with thorn bushes, making it an unpleasant exercise in sometimes painful bushwhacking. The path may be reinstated in the future but until then the easiest descent is to reverse your steps the whole way back to **El Masserof**.

The line of the southern ridge stretches away in front; it is possible to continue along this but the going is hard and you need to reverse your steps to descend.

WALK 14
Serra Ferrer North Ridge

Start/finish	El Masserof, near Xalo
Distance	8km
Grade	Moderate/Strenuous scramble
Time	4hrs
Terrain	Mountain tracks and a narrow, very exposed ridge
Height gain	400m
Map	Serra de Bernia (Terra Firma)/Costa Blanca Mountains (Discovery)
Access	From Xalo take the CV 749 signed to Bernia for 5.5km to El Masserof.
Parking	Roadside parking in the hamlet or just beyond it.
Note	Although not the most technically difficult ridge in this book, this is certainly one of the most serious. The early part of the ridge includes an extremely exposed narrow crest with long drops on either side and is suitable only for experienced scramblers with a good head for heights. If in any doubt use a confidence rope. To be avoided in windy or wet conditions.

The Serra Ferrer is far from the best known of the ridges of the Costa Blanca. In fact it is rather neglected compared with its more eye-catching neighbour, the Bernia, and with a reputation for being inaccessible. Yet it is among the very finest in the area. However, it comes with a serious health warning and the northern section includes a knife-edge crest that is no place for the uninitiated nor the nervous. Viewed from the Bernia or the Coll de Rates road it is a commanding sight that cannot be ignored, with a precipitous west face that can leave no walker or mountaineer unmoved. Sooner or later, one way or another, you just have to get it out of your system. Or see Walk 13 for an easier alternative.

With your back to the Verd i Vent take the dirt road by the black and white chevrons warning sign just to the north (right) of the Casa Susi Restaurant. This departure from the tarmac road is completely unmarked but a couple of minutes up the track a low mountain biking sign 'Solo experts' points off rightwards. Follow this down into a dip and then turn off left still following the signed mountain bike route as it traverses across the hillside. When it meets a road, turn right down the tarmac to reach a

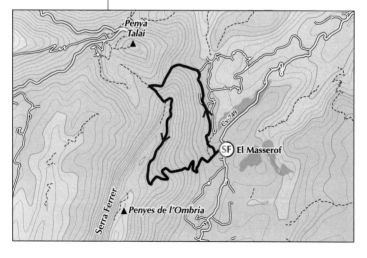

group of houses, one with an impressive array of solar panels. Turn left uphill opposite this following a sign to Esel Gestut. Carry on, passing the entrance to a donkey sanctuary and at the apex of a right hand hairpin bend where the road turns downhill go straight ahead on a narrow path marked by a cairn.

The track follows red paint spots across the hillside to enter a barranc, climbing steadily around the end of the ridge to a farm and well-tended olive groves. At a T-junction of paths just below the farmhouse turn left, ignoring the large red arrow on the opposite side of the barranc, which marks a route to the Coll de Rates (Walk 18). This next section is brutally steep, initially hurling itself directly up the slope, but in the upper section is does relent and zigzag a little following the occasional cairn still heading more or less directly up to the ridge.

The **crest** gives you a chance to regain your breath as you admire views ahead out to the coast with Olta, the Penon and Montgo behind you while the Puig Campana, Ponoig and Xanchet stand out with the Carrascal de Parcent nearer to hand.

Exposed scrambling above large drops on the Serra Ferrer North

This is the start of the most serious part of the ridge, which briefly involves walking along the very crest with large drops to either side. ◄ The most demanding section ends at a col, which, with the worst now behind you, makes a handy refreshment stop.

This is no place for those who suffer from vertigo.

From here continue along the line of the ridge but now following a path that traces a much easier and less exposed line, initially along the eastern flank just below the top. The track switches from side to side of the ridge, marked by paint dots, before dropping to a deeper col and then continuing past a large prominent pine heading towards an apparent maze of pinnacles ahead. It traverses the slope, slightly losing height to arrive at the foot of a pinnacle and crosses once again to the eastern (Masserof) side of the ridge, the way still marked by orange and red dots, to follow a rough path along a narrow shelf directly below the crags and aiming for the col ahead. This is the gap that divides the northern and southern halves of the Ferrer. When it reaches a broad track coming up from the valley turn left down this and follow it all the way back to **El Masserof** at the end of a very satisfying mini-adventure. ◄

It is possible to take in the southern end of the ridge for comparatively little extra effort by following Walk 13 from where it reaches the col at the broad track coming up from Masserof.

WALK 15
Cau Ridge

Start/finish	Car park by the Lady Elizabeth Senior School, near Xalo
Distance	13km
Grade	Moderate
Time	3 to 4hrs
Terrain	A broad ridge and a deep barranc
Height gain	525m
Map	Serra de Bernia (Terra Firma)/Costa Blanca Mountains (Discovery)
Access	From the N332 take the CV 750 towards Xalo. After 3.2km turn left up a steep tarmac road that quickly becomes concreted and leads to the Lady Elizabeth Senior School.
Parking	Signed car park just above the school.

The Tossalet del Castellet casts a long, lazy arm north eastwards into the Xalo Valley, or to give it its proper name the Vall de Pop. This green spur, reminiscent of a Lakeland fell, is known to walkers as the Cau Ridge and forms the natural bulwark between the mountains and the coast. Its position overlooking the coastal highways makes it one of the most accessible walks from the major traffic arteries.

Take the concrete road marked with a yellow arrow heading uphill just above the car park and carry on when it becomes unmade. It curls up the eastern side of the ridge and degenerates into a narrow path following the crest.

The spur climbs steadily with views of the coast and Penon at Calp in the east and up the valley to the double summit of the Penyo Roig and Cavall Verd and the surrounding serras to the west while Montgo dominates the view to the north. As it climbs the views ahead take in the end of the Bernia, the Puig Campana, Xanchet and the neighbouring serras.

The gentle Cau Ridge

The over-sized trig column crowning the Cau Ridge

After several false summits the 724m high top of **Tossalet del Castellet** finally comes into sight with an impressive triangulation point sitting atop a large square plinth out of proportion to the hill's relatively modest height or significance.

From the **trig point** it is possible to look down to the right and trace the path which will be the return route down the Barranc de les Gadiretes, while towards the coast the views take in Montgo, across Moraira to the Penon, Olta, the Mascarat Gorge and the Bernia. Around the horizon the Puig and other giants are laid out before you.

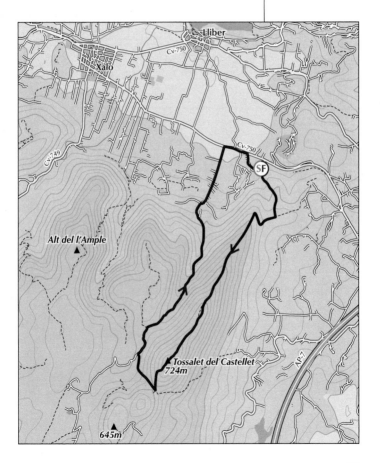

As the path drops down the inland side of the ridge the developments of the coast disappear and the atmosphere becomes one of mountains, terraces and olive groves.

Leaving the summit carry on along the ridge, guided over limestone slabs by a chain of cairns. At one point the path appears about to plunge over a precipice but a closer inspection reveals an easy natural rock staircase. ◄

At the col just above a set of rough cast agricultural buildings the main path goes left but look out for a pair of cairns which indicate a fainter track breaking away rightwards to skirt some pines. Follow this as it curls rightwards round the hillside. Where it meets a path coming from the left follow it rightwards downhill. At a T-junction with a broader track again go right. At the next T-junction, this time with a tarmac road, again head right. The road climbs slightly past a small casita and where it reaches a dirt turning area at the end of the tarmac go straight across to take a narrow path through the scrub. It weaves through thorns and gorse until the appearance of Montgo ahead signals that you have crossed the watershed and are on the homeward leg.

As the barranc steepens and deepens the path moves onto the right hand side of the valley for a long section of gradual descent through spiky undergrowth, dropping down abandoned terraces before the path finally enters a more amenable section through pine trees.

Shortly afterwards the path reaches a gravel road leading downhill. At a T-junction carry on straight ahead passing a green electricity sub-station and large villas to eventually reach the **CV 750**. Turn right along the road, taking care with traffic, to reach the junction taken earlier to the school and car park.

WALK 16

Alt de L'Ample

Start/finish	Xalo
Distance	12km
Grade	Moderate
Time	3 to 4hrs
Terrain	Hill paths, an avoidable scramble and a steep descent
Height gain	410m
Map	Serra de Bernia (Terra Firma)/Costa Blanca Mountains (Discovery)
Access	From the N332 take the CV 750 to Xalo. After the first roundabout turn left immediately before the petrol station into the Camino Cementario.
Parking	By the school or roadside parking nearby.

The series of ridges that tumble down into the valley near Xalo are among the most accessible from the N332 coast road. This route climbs to the top of Xalo's own mountain and is rewarded with a rock-girt summit whose final few metres are won only via a short scramble but which is a magnificent viewpoint from which to review the surrounding hills and coastline and to appreciate the contrasting geography of the northern section of the Costa Blanca.

Walk up the Camino Cementario past the small cemetery and houses to a T-junction and turn left onto the **CV 749**. This is a relatively quiet road but it is still necessary to take care and walk on the left to face oncoming traffic. The road crosses the barranc twice and just after the Kilometre 2 sign take an unsurfaced track on the left marked PR-CV Cases de Bernia. Follow this round bends for a little over a kilometre until just after a left hand bend it starts to drop into a barranc. Here leave the road and take a rising track on the left marked by a cairn and yellow and white marker paint on a pole supporting the power lines.

As you leave the treeline, the double summit of the Penyo Roig and the Cavall Verd Ridge can be seen; as you turn a corner the Bernia Ridge then comes into view.

Cross a flat area and carry on climbing up a now narrower path by the barranc. Where the path crosses the now quite shallow barranc continue on the main track, ignoring one climbing more steeply leftwards. The track passes a ruined casita and continues to climb through the pine trees. ◄

When the track nears the ridge a large cairn marks a narrow path heading off leftwards into the undergrowth and towards a rounded top. Along the way it passes a ruined casita daubed with direction markings. Having escaped the attention of the prickliest bushes the path contours around to another ruined casita perched above a staircase of terraces plunging down into the Barranc del Cau. Both are stark reminders of the almost unimaginable effort and hardship that in previous centuries went into wresting a precarious existence from this harsh and inhospitable terrain.

Steep terraces on the descent from the Alt

Turning a corner just beyond the casita the top of **L'Ample** appears, seemingly impregnable behind a rocky crown of crags. The last few metres involve a scramble up a polished groove. It is not as hard as it looks, nor

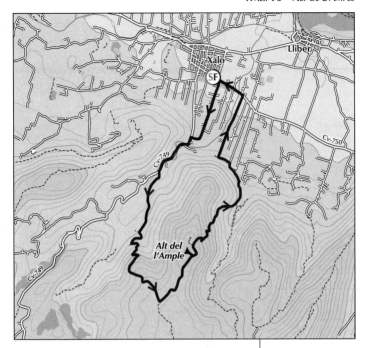

is it essential to climb it to appreciate the wide-ranging views, although the rim of the summit is a useful grandstand from which to pick out the line of the descent path. However, before committing to it remember that you will have to climb back down it to escape.

From the top reverse the scramble and return to the col. Go back along your approach path for about 100 metres to where, as you descend a small section of collapsed terrace marked with red and blue paint, you turn left down a path marked with occasional blue and yellow spots. It soon passes yet another ruined casita. The path is occasionally faint and at times quite eroded and loose as it criss-crosses the slope in a series of countless zigzags.

Finally as the path nears the mouth of the barranc it enters pinewoods and the going underfoot becomes easier as it curls round the foot of the ridge towards Xalo, passing above villas and houses. At a junction ignore an opportunity to go downhill but carry on at the same level until a couple of hundred metres further on a narrow path marked with a blue spot descends, which quickly reaches a surfaced road. Go straight ahead to reach the main road where you turn left into **Xalo**, again taking care with traffic on these last few hundred metres.

WALK 17

Carrascal de Parcent

Start/finish	By the junction of the CV 715 Coll de Rates road and the CV 720 on the outskirts of Parcent
Distance	15km
Grade	Moderate/Strenuous
Time	5 to 6hrs
Terrain	Mountain paths and broad stony ridge
Height gain	825m
Map	Serra de Bernia (Terra Firma)/Costa Blanca Mountains (Discovery)
Access	Leave the N332 on the CV 750 to Xalo. Go through Xalo and Alcalali and take the CV 720 to Parcent. At the junction with the CV 715 there is a Stoppomat.eu machine where cyclists can 'clock in' to time themselves on the fearsome 335m climb to the coll.
Parking	Roadside.

The Coll de Rates is rightly famed on the Costa Blanca. The views from the terrace of its restaurant are outstanding while determined cyclists and runners enjoy testing themselves against the gruelling 7km climb from the village of Parcent. However, walkers can go even higher as the col is merely one end of the broad ridge of the Carrascal, which throws a huge protective 950m high arm around the community that takes its name. This circular walk makes use of a modern PR-CV path and old trading routes to traverse the ridge.

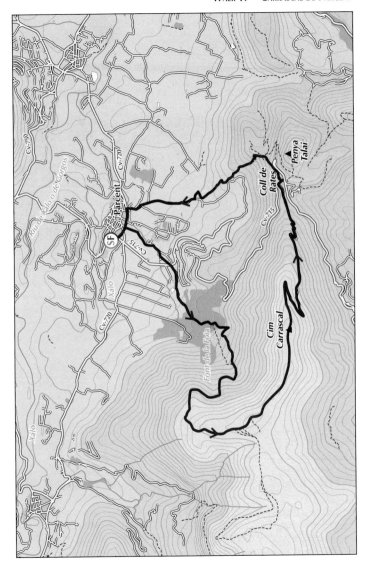

Lone tree on the approach to the ridge

Set off back down the CV 720 and after a couple of hundred metres, just past the Bodega de Parcent, there is a side road off to the right signed to Barranquet with a yellow and white paint marker. Take this. At the first bend after 100 metres leave the road and take an unsurfaced track into a dry streambed. Follow this until the way is blocked by a huge fallen tree then climb the left hand bank and follow the unsurfaced road that leads to a bridge on the Coll de Rates road. Cross the road to take a concrete track still running parallel to the dry river. The road weaves past houses and stables as far as the last house, where it becomes a narrow path continuing uphill.

After almost an hour of steady climbing it reaches a concrete road. Turn right along this to begin a long section of contouring and rising traverses, always heading northwards towards the end of the ridge. Along the way the road passes the **Font de la Foia** and immediately after it a yellow and white signpost directs you rightwards along the PR-CV 158 to the Caseta Forestal 4.8km away.

As you look back you can see the length of the ridge as far as the Coll de Rates with its restaurant; to the north the massif of Montgo squats in solitary splendour.

When the path reaches a junction by a wooden sign pointing to the Cava de Neu turn right to continue traversing. ◀ As the path reaches the final slopes it divides and becomes less distinct but the way is never in doubt. Simply keep pressing upwards making for the skyline. As you rise towards the ridge the hanging valley to the right dramatically reveals the limestone bands that form this mountain.

When the path finally breasts the ridge the views open up to the south to take in the length of the Bernia, the Puig, the Ponoig, and the spires of Xanchet, onwards to the double summit of the Cavall Verd and on round to Montgo. The ridge begins as a broad-backed stony desert with the indistinct path marked by occasional steel posts topped with yellow and white signs. The next section becomes sharper and those determined to walk this rocky tightrope will stick to the crest while those who prefer things a little easier will find a path down to the right.

After leaving the summit the path passes a pair of antennae and a relay station. The going becomes a little smoother after passing a forestry lookout tower, a reminder of the constant risk of fires in these hills. Follow the tower's concrete access road that zigzags all the way down to the restaurant on the **Coll de Rates**. ▶

At the turn off to the restaurant is another automated Stoppomat machine, which allows cyclists to time their ascent of the famous Coll de Rates route. Just behind it a track heads off down the hill, cutting out a loop of the road. At the bottom cross straight over the tarmac to take the PR-CV 158 signed to Parcent pel Cami de la Pansa.

The **Cami de la Pansa** weaves downhill revealing occasional remnants of cobbling and stepping that was once part of a Mozarabic trail used to export raisins – the pansas of the path's title – from Tarbena on the other side of the col. Before the coming of the modern road this was the main route across the mountains. This once-essential network of paths gradually fell into disrepair, a process hastened by the use of trail bikes and quads, but some were still in use up to the 1970s. Their value for recreational walking and tourism is belatedly being recognised and many are becoming signed and brought back into use.

The restaurant boasts that it is open every day and it makes a handy refreshment stop to allow your knees to recover.

As you near Parcent you pass the Pou d'Assagador, one of a chain of old wells along drove trails used to move sheep around the area in the Middle Ages.

As it descends the path crosses several other tracks, some broader, some narrower. Ignore them all and continue downhill making for the distinctive tower of Parcent church guided by yellow and white markings as the path wanders through orange groves and woods. ◄ When you reach the road turn left to soon pass the track to the riverbed used at the start of the walk back to the car.

WALK 18
Penya Talai (Rates)

Start/finish	Xalo
Distance	12km
Grade	Moderate
Time	4hrs 30mins to 5hrs
Terrain	Good paths
Height gain	585m
Map	Serra de Bernia (Terra Firma)/Costa Blanca Mountains (Discovery)
Access	On CV 750 in Xalo.
Parking	Riverside car park by CV 750 (closed for market on Saturdays).
Note	The walk starts from Xalo where there is ample parking but those who wish to avoid the lane at the start could drive to the end of the tarmac where there is very limited parking, saving about 90mins or so.

The Penya Talai, until recently known as the Penya Rates, presides over the pass whose name it used to share and could be reached much more quickly from the roadside there. However, this shapely peak deserves better treatment and taking the shortcut would miss out a delectably pastoral stroll through vineyards and olive and almond groves as well as two dramatic barrancs.

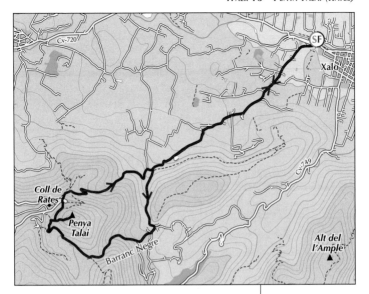

From the eastern end of the car park cross the road and take a narrow lane between the two popular cafés, the Aleluya and La Teulera. This is the Cami Tarbena but anyone hoping to drive to that village would be terribly disappointed. The tarmac ends after three delightful kilometres at a tiny parking area. ▸

From the end of the tarmac follow the continuation of the track leftwards between a shallow barranc and a retaining wall. Within a couple of hundred metres it comes to a junction by a natural bridge over the end of the barranc. The continuation of the path will be our return route so instead turn left up another broad track, which begins to rise. It climbs steadily up the deeply incised **Barranc Negre**, overgrown with scrub oaks and pine with the gable end of the Serra Ferrer framed in the head of the valley. Eventually the path comes to a more level section before reaching a working farm with well-tended terraces. Pass to the left of the farm to reach a narrow lane and turn right up this, passing a white casita

If you choose to shorten the walk and bring your car here take care not to obstruct the working areas.

This path is the same one used in Walk 14, the Serra Ferrer North.

and climbing to a sharp left hand bend where a faint track marked by a cairn heads off rightwards. ◄

Enjoy the pleasant climb, initially through trees and then clinging to the slope of the barranc, to pass through a wilder landscape with the rocks and crest of the Penya Talai above the opposite slope. Eventually it reaches a white painted farmhouse presiding over neat olive terraces.

At a T-junction of paths below the farm turn right to cross the barranc guided by painted red arrows on the opposite bank. The path soon becomes much less distinct on the broken rocky slopes but is guided by an abundance of red paint to arrive on a hairpin bend in an unmade road. Take the right hand option, heading uphill with the fire watchtower of the Carrascal de Parcent ahead.

After a few hundred metres as the track makes a sharp right hand bend just before the restaurant of the Coll de Rates comes into sight, look out for a tiny parking area carved into the hillside on the right with a path climbing up the slope from its rear towards the Penya.

Climbing towards the Coll de Rates. Serra Ferrer behind

It comes to a junction where scramblers may go straight ahead on a fainter path to pick their own route up the crags. Walkers may prefer to take the right hand and clearer option which climbs simply, if steeply, up the flank of the hill to the rocky summit of **Penya Talai**.

> From the isolated position of **Penya Talai** the views are superb in all directions, taking in the whole of the Vall de Pop and out to the coast with the Penon de Ifach and the Serra Olta, while nearer to hand is the Ferrer. In the middle distance are the towers of Benidorm and the Bernia. Further on Xanchet and the Ponoig stand out before the panorama comes back round to the Carrascal, the Cavall Verd Ridge and Penyo Roig.

To descend follow the path back down to the dirt road and then carry on round to reach the **Coll de Rates** and its welcome restaurant. This is open most days but it would be unwise to rely on it entirely, especially if you have to walk all the way back to Xalo. At the turn off

Parting of the ways. Signpost for green and white path below the Coll de Rates

to the restaurant is an automated Stoppomat machine, which allows cyclists to time their ascent of the famous Coll de Rates route. Just behind it a track heads off down the hill, cutting out a loop of the road. At the bottom cross straight over the tarmac to take the PR-CV 158 signed to Parcent but after a couple of hundred metres at a signpost turn right along the SL-CV 119 signed to Xalo 5km.

The path zigzags pleasantly through trees on a broad track down a barranc with abandoned terraces in its upper reaches before weaving its way down to meet the end of a tarmac road stretching away leftwards. The route, however, turns right along a wide unmade track across olive terraces. At the end of these it turns sharp left, following the edge of the cultivated area to quickly reach a junction of paths by a wooden post with several mountain bike signs on it. The main track appears to go straight ahead but instead turn back sharply right, the way signed by green and white paint to cross the natural bridge over the barranc passed on the way out and follow the track leftwards and within a couple of hundred metres regain the tarmac at the end of the lane from Xalo used on the outward leg. Follow it back to the town either on foot or by car, depending where you parked.

WALK 19

Penyo Roig

Start/finish	Murla
Distance	5.5km
Grade	Moderate
Time	4hrs
Terrain	Woodland paths and steep mountainside with sketchy tracks and a high ridge
Height gain	500m
Map	Serra de Bernia (Terra Firma)/Costa Blanca Mountains (Discovery)
Access	From Xalo take the CV 750 past Alcalali and at a T-junction turn right on the CV 715 before turning left shortly afterwards on the CV 719 to Murla.
Parking	Large car park at entrance to village.

The sharply pointed limestone summit of the Penyo Roig is the true eastern end of the Cavall Verd Ridge (Walk 20) but from that side the peak is defended by steep crags that make it the preserve of the serious scrambler, at the least, and some would say the rock climber. For walkers a much more amenable approach is up the eastern flank from the village of Murla, although even this is a rugged expedition that is likely to take longer than its comparatively modest length and height might suggest.

From the western edge of the village on a sharp left hand bend look out for an information board that marks the start of the PR-CV 426.

> This is also the start of a **Calvary** – the Stations of the Cross, each in its own white shrine, depicting key points in Christ's Passion and Crucifixion and a route of pilgrimage on the way to the Ermita de Sant Sebastia, which is passed on the walk.

Stations of the Cross climbing out of Murla

Walk up the concrete road passing the shrines and at the top climb the path that zigzags up above them through the shrubs and pines. After about half an hour's easy walking from the road the path reaches the white-painted **Ermita de Sant Sebastia** with fine views of the village and surrounding hills. The path continues to climb,

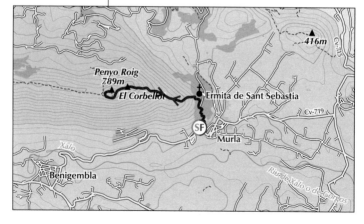

signed 'Cruz' (cross), a suspiciously precise 43mins away. Above the ermita the path becomes less distinct and when it leaves the trees becomes even less so as it clambers over bare rock, the route marked by cairns and the occasional flashes of yellow and white paint.

At the top of the slope it reaches a sign with a path marked off leftwards to the Cruz itself, a large metal lattice cross that crowns the subsidiary top of the Penya del Migdia overlooking the village 200m below.

Return to the signed junction and follow the arrow to the summit, which is now a further hour and a half away. As you climb the path becomes ever more indistinct, but still marked by paint flashes as it crosses rocky slopes and bare slabs. As it rises the ridge narrows and becomes much more sharply defined. At a gap the way appears blocked by a chimney but a red paint splodge points a cunning escape down to the right which allows the obstacle to be outflanked, opening the way to the first of the two summits, **El Corbellot**. From here the summit of the Penyo Roig is clearly visible beyond a rocky col.

The path initially follows the ridge before dropping down to the left, traversing below a line of protecting

Rocky ridge of the Penyo Roig

crags to reach the opposite ridge, which is climbed, still guided by the paint flashes to the summit of the **Penyo Roig**, and which proves to be a fine rocky vantage point.

The **view** has now opened up with the villages of the Vall de Laguar, Campell, Fleix and Benimaurell below and the cleft of the Barranc del Infierno (Hell's Gorge) beyond. It is just possible to pick out the steps of the Mozarabic trail climbing the distant slope and beyond them the series of summits and ridges fading away northwards towards Valencia. In the opposite direction is the village of Benigembla, the Carrascal and away to the right the sharply scalloped ridge of the Serrella.

To return to Murla it is easiest to retrace your steps since other routes involve rough descents over untracked ground followed by tedious road walking.

◄ In the initial section of the return leg make sure you drop down far enough to avoid the summit crags passed on the ascent. The nature of the terrain means that the descent may well take you almost as long as the climb.

WALK 20
Cavall Verd Ridge

Start/finish	Fleix
Distance	12km
Grade	Moderate with a little scramble
Time	3 to 4hrs
Terrain	Hill paths, narrow ridge and a little scrambling
Height gain	420m
Map	Serra de Bernia (Terra Firma)/Costa Blanca Mountains (Discovery)
Access	Fleix is one of the highest villages in the Vall de Laguar. From the N332 head through Xalo and on past Orba and Campell. Follow the signs for Vall de Laguar and Benimaurell to reach Fleix.
Parking	By the Ajuntament (Town Hall) of Fleix.

The Cavall Verd, also called the Caballo Verde, is a place where history, myth and legend intermingle. It is where the Moors who once ruled the Costa Blanca made their last stand in 1609 when the Spanish Crown ordered their final expulsion from the country. It is said that as many as 20,000 men, women and children retreated to this final stronghold. A Moorish warrior, the Green Knight who gives the serra its name, is said to have charged the Spaniards but in vain. The Moors were defeated and some histories have the survivors deported to North Africa from Denia. Darker versions say they were slaughtered on the hillside. What is in no doubt is that the ridge is one of the most enjoyable walks on the Costa Blanca. The valley is famed for its cherries and is particularly lovely during the April blossom season.

From the car park at the upper (western) end of Fleix walk a couple of hundred metres uphill towards Benimaurell and then turn off rightwards on a track, the CV 147 to Juvees d'Enmig. This leads down past the old communal washhouse and then begins to climb towards the brightly-painted houses of **Benimaurell**. When it enters the village take a flight of steps heading left and work

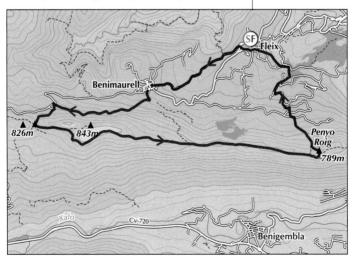

Walking along the ridge

your way up through narrow streets to the square by the church. Leave it by the Carrer del Pou and take the second left into Carrer del Princep. At the top of the hill a concrete track leads out towards the ridge.

After 250 metres take a path on the right, signed 'PR-CV 181 Coll de Garga'. This follows old steps as it traverses below the crags with views back to the village and the gorges traversed by the 10,000 Steps (Walk 22). When the path reaches a road turn uphill for a few paces before taking a path on the left, still the PR-CV 181 Coll de Garga. Within a few more steps the path arrives at a house and turns uphill following a broad track to reach a col where the views open up into the valley and the mountains beyond. Turn left following the signs to Cavall Verd 4.3km.

The path takes the south side of the ridge through pine trees and dwarf palms with your feet kicking up the scent of wild herbs. The town of Benigembla appears below while the ridge becomes broader, leading the eye towards the two rocky pinnacles at its eastern end.

Eventually the path becomes rockier and the going a little slower until it drops down to a col that offers an escape route to Benimaurell. The ridge, however, continues to Cavall Verd another 2km away and the real fun begins. It becomes increasingly narrow forming a rocky tightrope between the two valleys as it weaves its way between pinnacles with the occasional bit of scrambling thrown in. There is also a short downclimb, protected by a rope and equipped with a large metal staple step.

The path ends at a col where it is confronted by the steep buttresses of the **Penyo Roig** and moves into the domain of the serious scrambler. Walkers must admit defeat and turn leftwards down a steep and eroded path, which itself demands care. It zigzags precariously down through the terraces to meet a broader track, which is followed leftwards downhill. It comes to a crossroads and goes diagonally left to take a narrow path with yellow and white markers which continues downhill to meet a concrete road leading downhill. At a T-junction turn left and within 90 metres come to a signpost. The main track goes to Benimaurell. The path to Fleix turns off half right and then immediately bears right downhill on a narrow path by the edge of a wood. Cross a road and carry on downhill. Where it reaches a second road turn left. Keep

End of the road. Cliffs of the Penyo Roig force a return to the valley

following the yellow and white markers and at a junction on a bend go left towards some gates, still guided by the painted markers. The path appears to be about to enter the grounds of a house but before doing so it drops rightwards down into the woods and almost immediately crosses another track to curl round below the house. It ends on a flight of steps. Turn uphill and into **Fleix**.

WALK 21
Collado de Garga

Start/finish	Collado de Garga
Alternative start/finish	Near PR to CV 181 sign, 3km on from Collado de Garga
Distance	6km
Grade	Easy/Moderate
Time	2 to 3hrs
Terrain	Stony tracks and unsurfaced forest roads
Height gain	275m
Map	Serra de Bernia (Terra Firma)/Costa Blanca Mountains (Discovery)
Access	From the N332 head through Xalo and on past Orba and Campell. Follow the signs for Vall de Laguar and Benimaurell. From there continue another couple of kilometres up the valley to the bar on the Collado de Garga. For the alternative start/finish point, carry on over the col for another three serpentine kilometres to a PR-CV 181 sign on the right hand side of the road. There is parking for a few cars off the road a little further on. Immediately afterwards the road deteriorates markedly. The same spot can be reached from the Benigembla side of the hill by taking the CV 720 from Benigembla towards Castells de Castells. Immediately after a bridge 4km from Benigembla take a concrete road on the right. However, it is in very poor repair and those with a respect for their vehicle may find it more harrowing than anything met on the walk.
Parking	By the bar.

The Cavall Verd (Walk 20) is one of the classic walks and easy scrambles of the Costa Blanca. This shorter and easier outing flirts briefly with the main ridge and offers some similar views but with considerably less effort or difficulty. Its relative shortness makes it an ideal half day, perhaps combined with a leisurely lunch.

With your back to the bar turn left back along the road towards Benimaurell and after 100 metres take a path branching into the trees on the right, signed by yellow and white paint flashes. Follow it through the trees to a concrete road. Turn right up this for a few paces until, just before it reaches some farm buildings, fork left to follow the marked path heading up the slope.

The path traverses easily across the hillside with spectacular views down to the great cleft of the Barranc del Infierno to arrive at a crossroads of paths on a col 700m from the Collado de Garga. Confusingly, all four

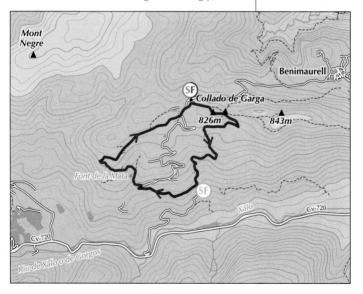

The water-worn stones of the Font de Mata

paths are marked PR-CV 181 with the left hand one heading towards the Cavall Verd itself. Our track, marked Font de la Carrasca, heads directly over the col and down the opposite slope, traversing first rightwards and then left downhill.

Where the track meets a broad, unsurfaced access road turn right along this for a few hundred metres following an intermittent wire fence on the left hand side. At the corner of the fence yellow and white flashes indicate the track going off leftwards downhill. If you miss this junction you will come to the road 100 metres further on.

The path drops steeply though pines and old terraces to reach an access track. Turn left along this, still following the flashes for 100 metres or so until, just before a dilapidated farmstead, the path turns right resuming its downhill course. It passes below a large crag before making a sweeping, gently descending traverse rightwards across the slope to the secluded but distinctly uninviting Font de la Carrasca. From here it continues downwards to meet another access road. Turn left downhill to join the tarmac road which has come down from the col. ▶ Turn right up this heading for the Font de la Mata 1.2km away.

This is the alternative start/finish point.

After about 10mins soon after a sharp right hand bend (not the track of the apex of the bend), a PR-CV 181 sign points the way off rightwards up the hillside to the **Font de la Mata**, now only a mere 300 metres away and the Collado de Garga.

> The **font** proves to be an elaborate structure and still very much in use. The initial section of channels is worn smooth by centuries of use, while the second section is more recently installed to serve the small terraces that are still cultivated. A large stone cistern supplies irrigation in the summer. The pitching of the path, which climbs away steeply, hints at its history as a trade route between the valleys.

The path briefly becomes concreted before joining a wider track. Turn left along it. When it reaches a farmhouse turn right up the side of it on a broad track, marked by flashes. Just beyond the buildings look out for a path heading off leftwards which is followed uphill through the scrub and across almond terraces to join a wider track, which is followed rightwards as it slowly becomes broader crossing the hillside towards the buildings on the *collado* to reach the tarmac road just below the bar.

WALK 22

10,000 Steps

Start/finish	Benimaurell
Distance	16km
Grade	Strenuous
Time	4 to 5hrs
Terrain	Mozarabic trails and lots of steps
Height gain	900m
Map	Serra de Bernia (Terra Firma)/Costa Blanca Mountains (Discovery)
Access	From the N332 go through Xalo, Orba and Campell. Follow the signs for Vall de Laguar and Benimaurell. As you enter the village a sign points to the parking area.
Parking	Village car park.
Note	None of the river crossings has a bridge so the walk is best avoided after prolonged or heavy rain.

There is more than a hint of the Grand Old Duke of York about this classic walk. It keeps marching you up towards the top of a hill and then marching you down again. It uses centuries-old Mozarabic trails to link three deep gorges and along the way racks up around 900m of ascent (and descent) without ever reaching a summit. That may seem heresy to hardened mountaineers, used to jealously husbanding every hard-won centimetre of height, but the wild scenery more than makes up for the effort and provides a route that will live long in the memory.

From the parking area walk back down to the entrance to the village and an information board. Go down a flight of steps leading to a concrete road which drops down to terraces and the old village well and *lavadero* – the washhouse where laundry was once a communal chore. These days the area is a picnic site with tables and a barbeque. The lane carries on for a little over a kilometre through cherry orchards and almond groves to reach the

neighbouring village of Fleix. As you stroll along the lane it is possible to make out the ascent path out of the gorge on the opposite flank.

Just before entering **Fleix** a footpath sign for the PR-CV 147 to Juvees d'Enmig signals the way forward, the start of the long descent to the Riu Girona. ▶

This staircase is the first of the Mozarabic trails. On the descent, about 15mins from the start of the steps,

The first of the 10,000 Steps descending to the Riu Girona

Before starting down the steps, it is worth taking a few steps further along the lane to visit Fleix's own restored washhouse.

If the steps get too much help is at hand – at a price

107

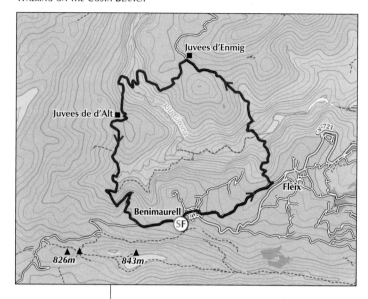

It is only as the path climbs that you appreciate the true skill of the trail builders and their cunning use of the slopes to ease the strain of ascent.

the path seems to be heading for a water slide. Do not be tempted by this as it leads to a 70m high waterfall. Instead go slightly leftwards to pass through an archway hidden in the rock and framing views of the remarkable path below. When the path reaches the riverbed, which is usually dry, savour these few flat paces before beginning the climb up the other side. ◀

As it climbs higher the trail forsakes the main gorge to enter an area of pines and scrub woodland before arriving at some almond groves with small huts and a well with a pump. This makes a welcome rest stop before continuing up the broad road still climbing away from the gorge. The road quickly crosses a small col and then passes two dilapidated houses. Just beyond them a sign points leftwards downhill to Juvees de d'Alt on the PR-CV 147. Take this path which in 100 metres reaches another house, where it turns left signed to Font Reina, Juvees de d'Alt, Barranc Infern and Benimaurell and is marked with yellow and white paint flashes.

A brief section through the trees ends as the path arrives on the lip of the gorge and begins its descent. This section, while still well-graded, is eroded in places and requires care. The scenery is now wilder than ever and as the path nears the bottom of the gorge it takes a long leftward traverse downstream to avoid crags below.

At the riverbed turn rightwards upstream for 100 metres or so to where the path climbs the opposite wall. At the top the path reaches **Juvees de d'Alt**, a collection of old huts, and the route turns right along the PR-CV 147 signed to Benimaurell. A couple of hundred metres further on by some ruined casitas the path turns off left, still the PR-CV 147 to Benimaurell now just 3km away. But they are quite some kilometres.

First comes the descent into the third and final gorge, the Barranc del Tuerto. As it crosses to the opposite wall views open up towards the sea, a reminder after hours of confinement that this is still the Costa Blanca. The final climb leads into an improbable-looking bay guarded by unbroken cliffs.

> The **staircase** writhes its way upwards before escaping to the left. Looking back it is impossible not to admire the workmanship of this superbly engineered trail which has unlocked the secrets of the gorges, working its way through the ravines and folds making use of every scrap of level ground and rendering the climbs if not effortless then at least surprisingly painless.

The path finally escapes the gorge and suddenly reaches the valley road, which leads leftwards downhill to **Benimaurell**.

WALK 23

Barranc de Racons or 5000 Steps

Start/finish	Fleix
Distance	12km
Grade	Moderate
Time	3 to 4hrs plus time to explore the gorges
Terrain	Mozarabic trails and steep narrow paths
Height gain	350m
Map	Serra de Bernia (Terra Firma)/Costa Blanca Mountains (Discovery)
Access	From the N332 head through Xalo on the CV 750 and on past Orba and Campell. Follow the signs for Vall de Laguar and Benimaurell.
Parking	Village car park.
Note	Since this walk makes use of quite a bit of the route of the 10,000 Steps (Walk 22) it is scarcely believable that they can offer such different experiences. This is definitely a walk on the wild side through impressive rock architecture demanding some route-finding ability, a steady head and a willingness to use a slightly precarious path. For most of the year the gorge is dry but it should be avoided after heavy rain or when rain is forecast.

Because this walk makes use of the start and finish of the 10,000 Steps some may feel it is worth doing only one of them. It really is worth doing both, but perhaps not on the same holiday. The 10,000 Steps is a classic Mozarabic trail and should not to be missed. However, the intimate exploration of the gorges on this route reveals an entirely new side of the Costa Blanca and is also a must for any adventurous walker.

From the parking area walk a couple of hundred metres up the road towards Benimaurell and then turn off right-wards on a track, the PR-CV 147, that leads down past the old communal village washhouse. Just beyond it take a track down to the right signed 'PR-CV 147 Juvees

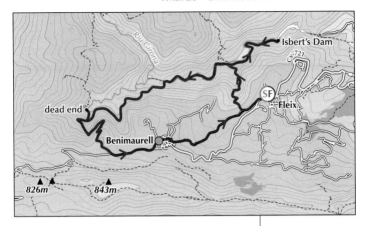

d'Enmig'. After about 15mins this passes through a rock arch and then carries on down well-engineered steps to the bed of the **Riu Girona**.

The main route lies leftwards (upstream) but before doing so head rightwards to not only extend the time in the gorge but also to visit one of the unwitting follies of the

Narrows of the upper Barranc de Racons

Costa Blanca. The dry riverbed twists downstream between high walls of orange and grey streaked limestone until after about 20mins it comes to a natural bottleneck plugged by the incongruous grey wall of **Isbert's Dam**.

> In this arid landscape where **water** is precious the opportunity to impound the winter rains that flow down the barranc was too good an opportunity to miss, especially when the natural narrowing of the gorge to just a few metres across meant that a quite small dam would hold back enough water to not only irrigate the land below but also slake the thirst of the local villages.
>
> Alas, nobody consulted the river and when the dam was completed and the time came to fill the newly-created reservoir the river declined to be taken prisoner. Instead it found a different route and seeped away through underground channels in the porous rock to continue its journey to the sea leaving the dam high and dry.

From this very definite dead end retrace your route to the foot of the steps and then carry on up the Racons over gravel and water-sculpted boulders like petrified waves. After about 20 to 25 mins from the foot of the steps the path passes through a section with larger boulders and oleanders before reaching a more open area with a natural narrowing ahead.

Here look for a pair of cairns on the left hand side with a faint orange paint splodge just behind them. This is the start of a faint and frankly unfeasibly steep-looking exit path. There is also often a cairn sitting on a low flat boulder in the middle of the streambed but this is vulnerable to storms and high water so is not always there. Should you miss the cairns your error soon becomes apparent as within a few minutes the path reaches a junction of gorges.

> It is worth exploring the rest of the **gorges** having noted the location of the exit path. After the

junction the left hand branch quickly becomes choked with boulders and thorn bushes. The right hand one, the Barranc de Racons, is a spectacular collection of dramatic, water-worn twists and turns. However, take care on the polished smooth rock which is quite slippery. Within 10mins or so, depending on water levels, you will reach the first of the pools and shortly afterwards the end of the road for walkers. Remember there is no pedestrian exit from either of these canyons other than the way you have come so you must be able to climb back down anything you decide to climb up to avoid becoming trapped. Rescue from here is difficult and there have been fatalities.

Wading through petrified waves. A walker makes his way up the dry Riu Girona.

At the twin cairns the path climbs steeply and at times is only faintly discernible as it crosses steep slopes to emerge after about half an hour onto a more open hillside above the wild-looking gorges. The track continues traversing and goes deep into the back of a gully before climbing out and round another one where the steps of a

Mozarabic trail appear coming down the opposite hillside (part of Walk 22). When the paths join, turn left and follow the welcome steps uphill to reach the road in about half an hour's steady climbing. At the road turn left into **Benimaurell**. Skirt round to the left of the village and just after the Pub L'Hedera fork left down a concrete road which becomes a quiet lane leading past the village washhouse, now a picnic area and barbeque, and on to **Fleix**.

WALK 24
Almadic Ledge Circuit

Start/finish	Benigembla
Distance	14km
Grade	Strenuous
Time	5hrs
Terrain	Good paths, slightly exposed; one tricky bit of navigation
Height gain	730m
Map	Serra de Bernia Marina Alta (Terra Firma)/Costa Blanca Mountains (Discovery)
Access	From Parcent take the CV 720 to Benigembla.
Parking	Layby 400 metres beyond Benigembla, opposite an information board for the PR-CV 427.

Although this delightful circuit of the Almadic Valley (sometimes called the Cordillera Ledge Circuit) reaches no summits and starts with some steep road walking it passes through very exciting terrain and is a match for any expedition in the book.

From the parking area walk back along the road and through Benigembla, crossing a roundabout towards Parcent. Immediately after crossing a bridge take a path on the right. When it reaches some overgrown terraces go up to the next level, which has been cultivated, and turn left between the trees to reach a metalled road.

Walk up the lane for a couple of minutes to where a concrete road turns off leftwards and climb steeply up this. At the first bend carry on climbing, ignoring a lane to the left marked 6 Almadic. Climb past houses and soon the rooftops of Benigembla are far below with the Almadic Valley opening up in front of you with the peak of El Mirabo across the valley.

At a left hand hairpin bend go straight on, following yellow and red arrows, as the path eases off and begins a gently-rising traverse above the valley. Continue past another house and then a communication tower on the right to arrive at a fork with a red arrow pointing left. Follow this, keeping to the main track and ignoring a track going right. Follow the main track as it curls round the shoulder of the hill to eventually pass another house with tall metal gates and superb views of the Cavall Verd Ridge and the double peak of the Penyo Roig across the valley. The now deteriorating path carries on up the slope for a few minutes until on a left hand bend a path marked by yellow arrows goes rightwards across the slope. Follow this.

Almadic Valley: the route traverses along the bands of cliffs on the left

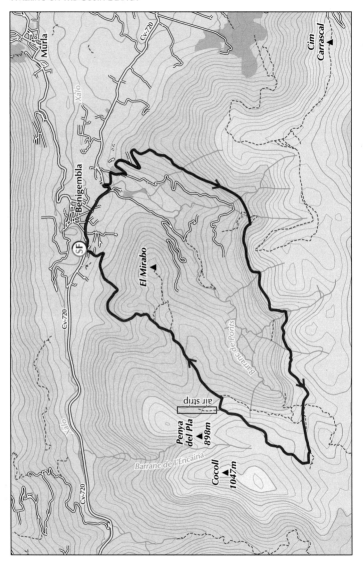

The path is initially sketchy in places but always reappears quickly as it contours across the slope to arrive on a promontory with views of the banded crags of the upper valley and the top of Cocoll easily identifiable at the valley head by its tower. The way ahead looks improbable but carry on contouring following the path. The next 90mins along the rim of the crags of the valley's southern slopes require little description since the terrain keeps you on the straight and narrow with prodigious drops at your right shoulder and the upper slopes of the mountain on your left. It is a pulse-quickening traverse, looping in and out of barrancs, constantly exhilarating while never really threatening.

After about an hour it passes a free-standing pinnacle and in another 30mins comes to a barranc with the remains of drystone walls. Cross this and climb up, heading up the valley side with Cocoll away to your right. Carry on into the next shallow barranc and climb out of this but where the main path begins to dip down into the valley head a little careful navigation and a bit of mountaincraft is required to pick your way through a maze of pathlets. If you keep in mind that the objective is to cross to the slopes of Cocoll and its improbably-sited airstrip to intersect a good path, the PR-CV 427, which descends to Benigembla from the runway, you will not go far wrong.

Where the path begins to descend look out for a very faint junction and take a faint track heading up the slope past a solitary low tree aiming for the rocky pyramidal top of Es Crestall and a pair of distinctive and almost identical trees on the col. The path is marked by the occasional dilapidated cairn. After a couple of hundred metres it comes to a path marked with red and white paint flashes. Turn left up this, climbing to a junction marked with cairns and red and white and yellow paint. Here turn right, traversing round the valley head.

The track passes through more trees to emerge in an open area below the Crestall, embellished with an impressive collection of almost a dozen old bathtubs and numerous upturned stones, which make handy benches for a refreshment stop.

Meanwhile look back to the outward leg and be astounded by the terrain you have crossed and perhaps appalled by the size of the cliffs you have been blithely wandering above.

Afterwards set off northwards up the slope, following a narrow unmarked path in the general direction of Cocoll. When it emerges onto more open ground the buildings of the **airstrip** and tower on **Cocoll** come into view and numerous paths pick their way between spiky shrubs. Your aim is still to intersect the PR-CV 427 and when you do so you will find it marked with yellow and white paint flashes and marker posts. Follow these rightwards. ◄

The path descends easily down a clear slope but remain alert and keep a sharp eye out for a small cairn and white and yellow cross on a stone beside the main track when you are just about level with the ridge of El Mirabo. Here turn right on the lesser track but still following the white and yellow flashes. The path initially clings to the ridge aiming for **El Mirabo** and a stand of pines but just after reaching them slips down to the left into the next barranc on a well-engineered, gently descending traverse which is a pleasure to walk even at the end of such a long day. It weaves its way down through terraces in about 45mins to arrive at the road opposite the parking space.

The contrasting second half: a broad valley with waymarked PR-CV

WALK 25
Barranc de Malafi

Start/finish	Pla de Petracos, near Benigembla
Alternative start/finish	Mouth of the ravine, near Pla de Petracos
Distance	20km; 9km for the barranc only
Grade	Strenuous; moderate for the barranc only
Time	5 to 6hrs; 3hrs for the barranc only
Terrain	Deep barranc and then a steep climb with clear paths but loose and stony
Height gain	640m; 80m for the barranc only
Map	Costa Blanca Mountains (Discovery)
Access	Take the CV 720 from Xalo towards Castell de Castells and pass through Benigembla, 6km later turn right signed to Pla de Petracos. If doing the whole circuit park in a large layby after 1.7km, near a sign marking the Petracos cave paintings. If doing just the barranc continue for another 2km to a walking sign at the mouth of the ravine.
Parking	Roadside laybys.
Note	This is rugged walking by anyone's standards with overgrown sections in the gorge so it is best to avoid wearing shorts or your favourite tee shirt. The paths over the Alfaro are steep and studded with sharp stones so good boots with solid soles are essential. Your feet will definitely know they've been for a walk.

Petracos is best known for prehistoric paintings on the caves above the valley but for walkers it holds another treasure, the magnificent Barranc de Malafi, which defines the northern edge of the lonely Serra de Alfaro. The whole circuit is a tough day and even though it is mostly on clear, broad tracks the going is hard, although the excellent views compensate for that. Rather like the Barranc del Cint (Walk 49) much of the pleasure is to be found in the grandeur of the opening section and a fine day can be had from an out-and-back trip through the gorge.

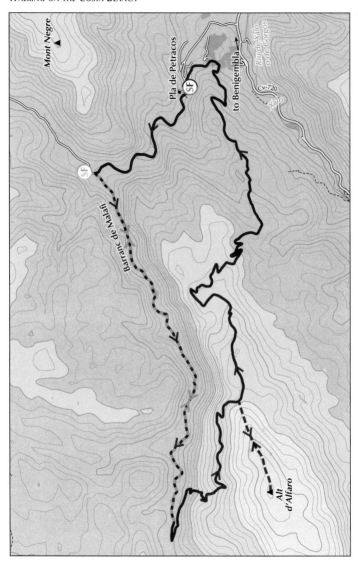

From the parking by the caves walk for 2km up the lane to the mouth of the barranc. As the road climbs its surface deteriorates but the scenery improves, becoming progressively wilder and more dramatic. The start of the **Barranc de Malafi** is marked by a PR-CV 168 sign. ▶ From this head into the barranc and, ignoring a track climbing into the olive groves, turn half left past almond trees to find a narrow path marked by a small cairn heading up the bed of the stream. The path continues, sometimes following the stream bed and at other times taking a more overgrown route along the sides.

Entrance to the Barranc de Malafi

This is the alternative start/finish point for the shorter version of the walk.

After 10mins it passes a small but well-maintained dam built to control flood water after storms. Above are huge vertical walls and pillars, initially to the left but later on both sides of the defile as it twists and turns, providing constantly changing views.

As it nears the head of the gorge aiming for large, square cut buttress on the left hand side the path reaches a fork. Go left, still following yellow and white paint

121

flashes to pass below the square tower. As it escapes the more confined section of the barranc the path comes into an open area with a PR-CV sign. A few metres further on it joins a forest track. Turn left along this, still following the bed of the barranc.

Barranc version only
If walking the barranc version only, turn back at this point and retrace your steps enjoying a new perspective on its huge walls.

The path passes a ruined casita and within a few minutes another track comes in from the right. Ignore this and carry on along the left hand branch, still aiming up the main valley. After another 5mins or so another broad vehicle track comes down from the left. Turn sharply up this, passing a decapitated road sign. It climbs steeply in a series of traverses and hairpins. When another track comes in from the right marked with a cairn ignore it and continue up the main track.

The path is so loose that sometimes it resembles a scree run and at others a riverbed. One can only wonder at the nature of the vehicles that have left their tyre marks along it. Finally it breaks out onto easier ground offering a perfect view of the length of the barranc below and the mountains beyond. Eventually it passes an incongruous bike and car road sign before curling round to a col.

Diversion to the summit of Alfaro
Those whose day is incomplete without a summit should look out, just after crossing the col, for a pair of cairns on the right which mark the start of a rough and uncomfortable path leading to **Alt d'Alfaro**. This will add 30 to 40mins to the day. Whether the reward justifies the discomfort of crossing sharp limestone flakes is debatable.

After the col keep following the track, ignoring a vehicle track that turns off leftwards, apparently heading towards the mouth of the barranc. This eventually loses itself in a confusion of hunters' and animal tracks and is easier to follow in ascent. So instead continue along the main track, which at first appears to be heading in the wrong direction. Eventually it becomes partially concreted. Carry on down it in a series of bends and at a T-junction turn left on an unmade track. It passes old corrals before swinging left to pass an impressively deep concrete-encased well. At the bottom of a steep slope where the concrete ends pass a large open water tank and go round another hairpin. At the bottom of the slope turn left along an unmade road that passes through almond groves. When it reaches a T-junction turn right for a few paces and then left down the signed PR-CV 168 to Tollos por Petracos.

In keeping with the rest of the walk, this is one of the rougher and less well-tended PRs. Pass below a recently renovated house to reach a dirt road, now liberally spattered with white and yellow paint. After a couple of hundred metres, as the track enters terraces, look out for paint flashes on the right indicating where the path cuts down the hillside to cross more terraces. Where it appears to vanish completely, it dives into the undergrowth to traverse the hillside above farms and houses to eventually arrive at the tarmac valley road. Turn left back to the car at **Pla de Petracos**.

Looking back down the length of the Barranc de Malafi

WALK 26
Serra Forada

Start/finish	Alcala de la Jovada
Distance	9km
Grade	Moderate
Time	3hrs
Terrain	Good tracks, rough ridge
Height gain	290m
Map	Costa Blanca Mountains (Discovery)
Access	The Vall d'Alcala is most easily reached from the east along the CV 712 from Pego and Vall d'Ebo. However, a very picturesque although narrow road also approaches from the south via Castell de Castells and Fageca.
Parking	By the swimming pool.

Among mountains riddled with countless holes or *foradas* it is a bold statement to declare any one of them to be 'the' forada but the archway visited on this walk not only claims that honour it actually gives its name to an entire range. That may be rather overstating its case but there is no denying it is a stunning natural feature and since it appears at the end of one of the Costa Blanca's most delightful ridges it would be churlish to argue too much. Alcala de la Jovada, once a stronghold of the Moorish leader, Al Azraq, is set in a wide bowl with no dominating peak hemming it in so the impression is of wide, open countryside, unusual among these mountains. The ridge can be approached from the north or south but this route has the advantage of quiet tracks and fine views southwards to the Serrella during the ascent. It starts from the swimming pool where there is also a bar.

Go back to the CV 712 and cross over following signs to La Vall campsite. Follow the metalled road past the campsite and carry on making for a road that can be seen winding up towards the ridge. Ignore side tracks until the road reaches a Y-junction. Here go right, signed 'A4 Cami del Corrals d'Andon'. Where the concrete track ends take

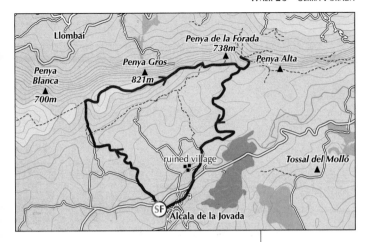

a path climbing leftwards and heading for the col through a broad valley with occasional almond groves. At the col the views to the north of the Vall de Gallinera open up with the villages of Benissili and Alpatro at your feet.

This is the start of a glorious ridge walk and the path climbs rightwards to a rock band and then makes a rising rightwards traverse beneath the face to reach a subsidiary summit from which the ridge can be seen curving away to the rocky crest of the Penya Gros with the cliffs of the northern escarpment dropping vertically into the Gallinera.

The track curls round the cirque before rising to the triangulation column of **Penya Gros** where you realise the summit is not actually part of the main ridge but sits atop a spur thrust out over the valley. To continue along the ridge, which stretches sinuously away to the sea, it is necessary to retrace your steps a short way and then contour round the head of a steep, crag-rimmed barranc. The ridge continues with the path sometimes easy to follow and sometimes easy to miss but the general line is never in doubt.

After an hour or so of sublime ridge walking a broad track can be seen arriving across the southern slope to

Looking south from the forada

The window is far from the largest on the Costa Blanca, dwarfed by, among others, the twin portals of Els Arcs (Walk 32) but what it lacks in diameter it makes up for in position.

join the main ridge path just before a small hut perched on the brink of the cliffs. This track is the descent route but before dropping down to join it follow the path round the ridge to find yourself suddenly confronted by the forada itself with fine views through the window back along the escarpment you have just traversed. ◄

To descend retrace you steps from the forada and then turn left to take the broad track coming up from the valley seen earlier. At a fork go right along a grassy track which passes through banks of gorse and the skeletal remains of trees destroyed in a major forest fire in 2008. At the next fork go left following the path over a small rise. When the track comes to a junction with a BTT cycling waymarker go right still following the wider track. At the next T-junction go right again, still aiming for the village. When it meets a concrete track turn left, passing the remains of the old Moorish settlement, still astonishingly well preserved, to rejoin the CV 712 back to **Alcala de la Jovado**.

INLAND FROM BENIDORM

During the summer months the electric boat runs on Guadalest reservoir (Walk 33)

WALK 27
Serra Gelada

Start	The northern end of Benidorm's promenade
Finish	Albir
Distance	10km
Grade	Strenuous
Time	3 to 4hrs
Terrain	Clifftop paths, steep climbs and descents
Height gain	1000m
Access	The walk goes from Benidorm to Albir so requires either two cars or the use of the regular No 10 bus between the resorts. The advantage of parking in Albir and taking the bus to start the walk is that your fate is then in your own hands and not reliant on the bus.
Note	Those who know only the gentle landward face of the Serra Gelada may be surprised to see it given such a serious rating but the mountain, at 438m a tiddler compared with the inland giants, packs a remarkable punch. Not only does the sea level start mean every centimetre has to be earned but the ridge itself is a rollercoaster of summits and gullies, demanding often rough and eroded ascents and descents along the way, adding up to more than twice its actual height.

If proof were needed that the coastal hills are not to be taken lightly it comes with this walk. It starts on the teeming beaches of Benidorm and ends by the rather more sedate sands of Albir but in between are wild seacliffs, dropping hundreds of metres into the Mediterranean. The walk can be tackled from either end but this version has the advantage of putting the tower blocks of Benidorm at your back for most of the way, allowing attention to concentrate on the natural grandeur that abounds.

From the northern end of Benidorm's promenade take a narrow alley that climbs beside the Hotel Nadal to a road. Turn right and follow it to the coast before it curls up between hotels and apartments. At the top of the first climb take the Calle Sierra Dorada. At a roundabout take the right hand fork signed to La Cruz (The Cross) and at the next bend the Cross, our first objective, comes into view. The tarmac ends after half an hour's stiff climbing, at a viewpoint just below the **Cross**. Continue along the

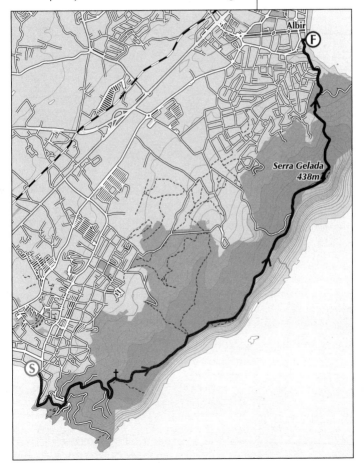

Benidorm's promenade, an unusual starting point for a walk

path and at a gap in the fence go through, following a dirt path towards the first summit, which is marked by a large cairn.

A maze of paths heads across the next level section but the way is never in doubt with Albir and the antennae on the final summit, coming into view and looking deceptively near. At the end of the level section the first glimpse appears of the towering cliffs below together with the first steep descent of the ridge. At the bottom of the slopes the path traverses the very edge of the cliffs and is no place for those of a nervous disposition.

The final summit before the antennae is crowned by a small concrete post while below the service road for the transmitter station appears but the rough path continues along the ridge.

Just before the station the path briefly joins the service road before, almost at the gates, a path marked with a white arrow on a metal post heads off left aiming for the rooftops of Albir far below. A multitude of rough paths wend their way downhill but follow the general direction of the power lines. By staying slightly to the right of the wires it is possible to pick up a track breaking rightwards and marked initially by red paint but later in almost every colour of the rainbow. The general rule of thumb when presented with a choice is to opt for rightwards and downhill. The paths eventually converge on a large parking area at the entry to the Parc Natural de Serra Gelada. From here carry on downhill to **Albir** and to wherever you parked your transport.

WALK 28
Head of the Algar Valley

Start/finish	Fonts de L'Algar, near Callosa d'En Sarria
Distance	11km
Grade	Moderate
Time	3hrs 30mins to 4hrs
Terrain	Forestry tracks and country roads
Height gain	470m
Map	Serra de Bernia Marina Alta (Terra Firma)/Costa Blanca Mountains (Discovery)
Access	From Callosa d'En Sarria take the CV 715 Bolulla road and shortly after leaving the town turn right signed 'Fonts de L'Algar'. Follow the road downhill to the river and the Bar La Cascada.
Parking	Spaces are at a premium at this popular tourist spot during peak season and out of season many are chained off. However, parking can usually be arranged at the Cascada if you ask and buying a pre-walk coffee also helps.

Fonts de L'Algar is popular with locals and visitors alike both as a beauty spot and picnic venue. However, this walk quickly leaves any crowds behind to provide a superb expedition into the upper reaches of the Algar Valley close under the massive cliffs of the Penya Severino and the Penya Ovenga, which more than justify the early road walking.

From the bar walk down the road between the building and the river and follow the lane which soon turns steeply uphill between fruit trees for a kilometre or so. At the top continue along a flat section to reach a three way junction by a power pylon. Take the right hand option, the continuation of the main road, heading into the valley and following yellow and white paint flashes.

After 3 or 4mins it reaches a fork. Take the right hand branch, dropping steeply down to the valley floor, eventually becoming a concrete road. On a sharp right hand bend next to a large overgrown boulder on the left hand side turn sharply back leftwards into a dry steambed. The boulder has a red painted arrow on its rear but, somewhat unhelpfully, this is not visible from the main track until you have made the turning. If you miss the junction and reach the metal gates of the Pouet de Sacos water works you have gone too far and should retrace your steps.

At first the rough and stony path seems to double back on itself to run beside the concrete road just descended but soon it veers off rightwards and becomes clearer and smoother. The early section follows the valley then begins to zigzag uphill. Having gained height the track levels out and contours round the head of the valley to reach the substantial ruins of the **Casa Pons** on

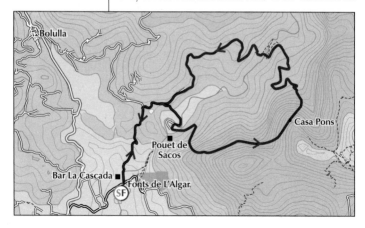

Paso de los Bandoleros closes the head of the Algar Valley

a promontory to the left of the track about 45mins from the valley floor. ▶

From here continue straight along the track as it passes another house and works its way round below the rocky cirque before winding back down to the valley. It crosses the riverbed before continuing up the opposite flank to reach yet more ruins on a T-junction of tracks. Here take neither branch but instead cross diagonally over to slip between the ruins and out onto cultivated terraces. Go along these to the end and then climb up a couple of levels to continue along them. When they emerge on a bend of a lane turn left downhill. The track leads easily down the valley affording plenty of opportunity to enjoy the rock architecture before arriving back at the three way junction reached on the outward leg. Here turn left and follow the road back to **Fonts de L'Algar**.

This is a good spot to take stock of your progress and to admire the superb setting perched high above the valley with the impressive cleft of the Paso de los Bandoleros behind.

WALK 29
Bolulla Castle

Start/finish	Bolulla
Distance	8km
Grade	Moderate
Time	3 to 4hrs
Terrain	Steep paths, some rough ground
Height gain	520m
Map	Serra de Bernia Marina Alta (Terra Firma)/Costa Blanca Mountains (Discovery)
Access	From Callosa d'En Sarria take the CV 715 to Bolulla. When just about to leave the village turn sharp left to park near the Bar Era.
Parking	Alternative parking on the other side of the CV 715.

This is one of those wonderful short walks with which the Costa Blanca mountains abound which prove that it is not necessary to climb for thousands of metres or march long distances to be among wild scenery and rugged mountains. It knits together ancient mule tracks once used to supply the castle with modern roads that serve scattered villas and cultivated terraces. The goal is the ruined castle that sits atop a rocky tower but the journey is every bit as exciting as the destination.

With your back to the Bar Era head up the concrete road opposite, uphill rightwards out of the village, passing houses and a large cistern, before dropping into a gorge and crossing the dry riverbed and continuing past more houses. Ignore all the side routes until past the last house which has an impressive array of solar panels. About 100 metres beyond the building take a track heading down into an orange grove. Just before it climbs into the fruit trees a cairn directs you onto a path in the dry stream bed.

This brief section has a Lost World feel about it with overhanging bushes and trees. Someone armed with secateurs or, better still, a machete could perform a great service to the walking community. Fortunately it is short, so press on, encouraged by occasional paint splodges on the rock.

After a couple of hundred metres it reaches a cairn perched on a rock and the path clambers out up the right bank and turns left along a track still heading into the gorge. When it reaches a wider track turn right up this for about 100 metres until a clear path marked by another cairn climbs leftwards into the trees. Follow this. ▶

When the track reaches a metalled road turn left up and round a bend and after 100 metres look out for a concrete road on the left, marked by yet another cairn. Ignore this for the moment but it is a crucial junction on the descent. For now, however, carry on up the road for another couple of hundred metres passing a large concrete drainage channel and then immediately after a short stretch of retaining wall reinforcing the embankment turn left up a path which almost immediately curls back right paralleling the road. After a few more paces at a left hand

Look up at the great rock on which the castle is perched and down to the huge vertical cliffs of the Paso Tancat (Closed Pass); a glance behind reveals the Bernia Ridge and the Severino.

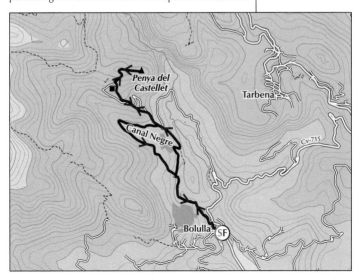

bend in the track a path climbs directly ahead, marked by a cairn, the occasional steps and pitching hinting at its history as the old mule track that once served the castle. When it meets another track turn right to quickly rejoin the surfaced road. Go left uphill for 100 metres to the next bend when a clear track climbs rightwards. This is the continuation of the mule path with some of the most obvious steps and pitching of the whole route as it climbs through olive terraces to arrive at the road head and a rough parking area.

> Any cars in the **parking area** are likely to belong to rock climbers visiting the crags below the castle. It is also used as the start of Walk 30, Bolulla Circuit/Raco Roig, but while driving to this point may take much of the effort out of the ascent, on this comparatively short walk it also steals much of the pleasure, not least the impressive rocky scenery of the Paso Tancat, which is not to be missed.

The house has been up for sale; if new owners take a dim view of walkers using their drive it could become necessary to skirt round the fence to reach the path.

Turn right up the now very rough road to a modern house opposite a ruin. The route to the castle begins from here. ◀ Leave the grounds of the house through the rear boundary. The going up to the castle is quite rugged and overgrown in places while other sections demand the ascent of short rock steps. Follow the richly cairned rough, track climbing towards the crags and then traversing below them to reach the ruins. All that is left of the castle itself are a few stunted walls but they are enough to appreciate its magnificently defensible position with its back to huge cliffs and steep slopes in front.

From the castle drop back down to the house and follow the track back to the parking area and then take the mule track used on the ascent to the next road, cross over and still following the ascent route take the path, taking care not to miss the junction on the left after a few metres. (The continuation of the broader track does not lead to the valley but ends in cultivated terraces.)

When the path reaches the road carry on down to the concrete road noted on the ascent and turn right down

this. Follow it as it crosses the barranc of the **Canal Negre** with more excellent views across to the Bernia. When it reaches a fork after about 15mins take the left hand branch and continue along this, ignoring all descending tracks until it reaches a four way junction about 5mins further on. Go straight on for a few steps to a cairn at the start of a path dropping off the terrace. Go down the slope to a pair of cairns by a large tree. This is the start of the final section of mule track, which is followed as it snakes downhill to arrive at a road. Turn right along this to soon pass the house with the solar panels and follow the outward route back to **Bolulla**.

Ruins of Bolulla Castle

WALK 30
Bolulla Circuit/Raco Roig

Start/finish	At the end of an unmarked side road above the village of Bolulla
Distance	8km
Grade	Moderate
Time	3hrs
Terrain	Mountain paths
Height gain	250m
Map	Serra de Bernia Marina Alta (Terra Firma)/Costa Blanca Mountains (Discovery)
Access	From Callosa d'En Sarria take the CV 715 towards Tarbena. After passing Bolulla the road climbs steeply. On a right hand hairpin bend take a narrow tarmacked lane heading leftwards on the crown of the bend. Follow this steeply uphill until the tarmac ends by an olive grove. Park here off the road.
Parking	Roadside. Do not obstruct the unsurfaced track, which serves houses up the mountain.

The village of Bolulla is best known for its castle perched high on a fin of limestone overlooking the Val de Algar (Walk 29) but this walk initially turns its back on that landmark and instead heads into some uncharacteristically gentle country before culminating with a jaw-dropping finale worthy of climaxing any walk.

Looking down the right side of the valley it is just possible to make out a natural rock arch in the crags near the top of the slope.

Set off up the broad track past a restored farm house and just before it reaches a col look out for a small cairn and red painted arrow marking a narrow path heading off leftwards across the terraces towards a small ruin. After an hour's steady climbing it arrives at a surprisingly broad and grassy col with old terraces. Continue along the path climbing the terraces until it drops down steeply through trees to the head of a small barranc, which makes a sheltered rest stop. ◀

From the head of the barranc take a narrow path, which sets off contouring along the left hand side of the valley with the arch becoming more prominent as you proceed. The path continues round until it reaches a more open bowl cultivated with orchards and almond groves. When it reaches a broader vehicle track carry on straight ahead along this with a large white house in

The start of the Bolulla Circuit with Bolulla Castle behind

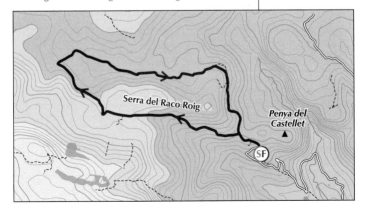

From the outside it is an unprepossessing structure with a small mesh door but a glance inside reveals it to be surprisingly cavernous and well built.

the distance. When it meets a tarmac road turn right and carry on down past a sign pointing the way to the well of the Aljub Xorquet on the PR-CV 151 passing more almond groves on the way. At a junction take the higher of the two tracks and look out for the well, which is sunk into the wall of the terraces to your right. ◀

Carry on along the track down the valley, ignoring a crossed white and yellow paint mark. This is designed to prevent those on the PR-CV 151 Els Arcs Circuit (Walk 32) going astray. The path continues round the barranc, passing more almond groves where it drops a level and becomes narrower as it crosses high above a barranc with a huge cave away to the left. It weaves through undergrowth in a very open landscape amid rolling hills, a marked contrast with the usual ridge and ravine walking on the Costa Blanca. At the end of the traverse the path climbs a gentle slope and after another flat section the walk becomes instantly and unexpectedly spectacular.

> The most stunning of **vistas** is suddenly presented as the path turns a corner. Before you, fold upon fold of rock and plunging ridges, a deep defile and the Castell de Bolulla perched on its rocky eminence. Beyond, the towers of the Serra de Bernia provide the perfect backdrop. Scenery simply does not get any better and it is all the more striking for the contrast with the rounded slopes that have filled the last hour.

The path carries on contouring across the right hand side of the valley with constantly changing perspectives on the cliffs opposite. It squeezes between trees and boulders before arriving at a flat area. Take a final look at the vast faces opposite before crossing the col to find yourself at the cairn marking the path taken at the start of the walk. Continue down the track back to the car.

WALK 31

Cim de Aixorta

Start/finish	Plans d'Aialt at an information board near the Km7 marker between Tarbena and Castell de Castells
Distance	17km
Grade	Moderate
Time	5hrs
Terrain	Mostly good forest roads, one steep climb and a steep descent
Height gain	525m
Map	Serra d'Aitana (Terra Firma)/Costa Blanca Mountains (Discovery)
Access	On the CV 752 either via Callosa d'En Sarria and Tarbena or from Castell de Castells.
Parking	By the information board.

The Serra Aixorta is a natural extension of the Serrella, although not quite so wild and untamed as its shaggy neighbours, a situation not helped by the over-exuberant pouring of concrete on the access tracks. However, once beyond the reach of the men with the mixers its natural ruggedness reasserts itself in a fine 1221m high rocky summit, a bit of bushwhacking across the southern slopes and a grand finale with as fine a pair of natural rock arches as you could wish to meet at the end of long day on the hill.

From the parking area, where a sign points to our first objective, the Font del Teixos 9km, walk up the wide track following the PR-CV 151 and signs for Els Arcs. It passes ruined houses but at a more modern building where the road becomes metalled turn left heading into a valley. At a T-junction turn right still on the PR-CV 151 signed to Els Arcs following the road as it climbs through cultivated terraces and a series of bends. The road becomes concreted, beginning a pattern of intermittent 'improved' sections, which have been increasing in number and length over the years. The farmers and foresters who use

The hanging valley and Aixorta

the road obviously prefer it but walkers may be less keen. However, it does allow height to be gained quite easily.

Where, after about half an hour, a sign points off to the right to Els Arcs carry on up the road signed Font del Teixos. As the road tops a rise the ridge of the Serrella comes into view with the great gouge of the Barranc de la Canal in the nose of the Mallada de Llop. After a couple of hairpins the concrete ends at a T-junction, on another bend. A sign points rightwards to the Font. However, we can shortcut this section of road by turning left up the all-too-obvious steep, stony track. A few minutes' hard pulling leads to a jaw-dropping exit into a magnificent hanging valley. ◀

Here Aixorta and the cliffs of the Penya Alta come into view while leftwards towards the sea the great jumbled wall of the Ferrer and end of the Bernia decorate the horizon.

Concrete is forgotten as you carry on along the grassy track passing two paths going off to the left. The main track curves rightwards to rejoin the road we climbed earlier and which is now followed uphill to a T-junction where a sign reveals the font to be only 3.3km away. We will return to this junction from the opposite direction on the descent, however, for now turn left and follow the track all the way to the font. This section passes directly

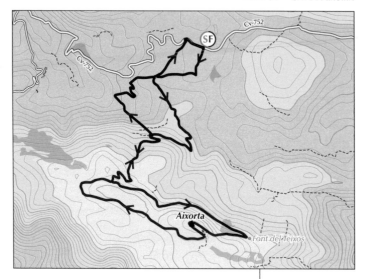

below the cliffs of the Aixorta, which are of constant interest being riddled with caves and pinnacles.

Font del Teixos is reached just after passing a large green fire fighting reservoir. There is a picnic table and a Hansel and Gretel-style house, which proves to be a climbers' refuge. ▶

Disappointingly, after all those signs, the water is apparently not suitable for drinking.

The Hansel and Gretel climbers' refuge

The path goes to the right of the refuge and climbs steeply to a col where Aitana comes into view beyond a cultivated little bowl. Turn right up the rocky slope, passing three large clumps of trees to reach the summit of **Aixorta** with fine views, especially along the ridge of the Serrella.

To descend return to the col and drop towards the fields but be certain not to enter or cross them. This is perhaps the most crucial bit of navigation on the entire walk and an error here could lead you towards Guadalest, not itself a disaster but it would result in either an embarrassing call for a lift, an expensive taxi fare and a very unwelcome trudge back uphill on tired legs so do not be lured into the barranc.

Instead contour rightwards across the slope and stay well above ruined buildings at the corner of the fields on a narrow path marked by occasional very unofficial-looking yellow paint sprays and crude arrows. The path clings tenaciously to the slope just below the upper rocks of the ridge sometimes rising or falling a little but with no dramatic changes in altitude. After about half an hour from the col it becomes broader and then turns the shoulder of the mountain and drops to a chained entrance at a T-junction with a forest track. Here turn right uphill and within a few minutes reach the junction passed on the ascent by the Font del Teixos 3.3km sign and a 30kph post.

Turn left down the route used in ascent going down the concrete road and then turning off right into the hanging valley and the steep and stony path used on the way up. At the foot of this turn right, still reversing the ascent route as far as the next right hand hairpin, where a narrow trod heads off leftwards, marked by a decapitated sign and two faded blue paint splodges, one on a tree on the left, the other on a boulder to the right. Take this path through the trees and after only about a minute go right at a fork and be prepared to stop very quickly indeed. Within a few paces it arrives at a completely unguarded viewpoint on the edge of a 10m drop which gives a birdseye view of Els Arcs, twin rock arches divided by a slender band of limestone (pictured in Walk 32).

Return to the fork and now take the other path, which leads steeply down to the foot of the highly photogenic arches. After admiring this natural phenomenon leave by the path going rightwards through a cultivated area and a forest road. Here turn left signed to Penya Escoda on the PR-CV 151. Carry on past a house to T-junction where you go right towards Plans d'Aialt. Continue to another T-junction marked with yellow and white paint. Here turn left down to the road and then right for the 100 metres or so to the parking area.

WALK 32

Els Arcs

Start/finish	Plans d'Aialt at the Km7 marker between Tarbena and Castell de Castells
Distance	7.5km
Grade	Easy
Time	2hrs to 2hrs 30mins
Terrain	Mostly wide tracks with a short narrower section to the arches
Height gain	200m
Map	Serra d'Aitana (Terra Firma)/Costa Blanca Mountains (Discovery)
Access	On the CV 752 either via Callosa d'En Sarria and Tarbena or from Castell de Castells.
Parking	By the information board.

This walk, scarcely more than a stroll and completed within a couple of hours or so, is nevertheless well worth doing for its fine views and to visit one of the most striking natural sights of the Costa Blanca. The two arches of Atancos, a 12m high natural bridge and its small brother just below it, have been eroded over millennia and are surprisingly difficult to spot from a distance but as you approach they reveal their full grandeur.

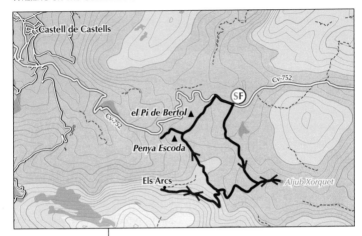

From the parking area walk up the wide track. It passes ruined houses but at a more modern building where the road becomes metalled turn left heading into a valley. On a bend a sign points a short diversion leftwards to the **Aljub Xorquet**, a protected well which is built into the terraces some 250 metres down the track.

> To visit the well, follow the signed diversion. At first sight the **well** seems insignificant with just a single small door but a glance inside reveals it to be cavernous and deep. Considerable work has gone into creating it, testimony to the importance of water on this high plateau. There is also a carved stone bowl and a drinking vessel on a long string to be lowered into the water. Retrace your steps to the sign.

Continuing around the bend, carry on up the road, still on the PR-CV 151 signed to Els Arcs. As it climbs through cultivated terraces and a series of bends the road becomes concreted and carries on to Font del Teixos (Walk 31). However, our route turns off rightwards along a level track signed Penya Escoda and Els Arcs. After a few hundred metres the track deteriorates into a narrow path and almost immediately reaches the signed diversion to Els Arcs on the left. The path winds through trees and curves round over terraces heading for the cliff face above. As the path climbs **Els Arcs** suddenly appear, framing the view of the distant mountains.

Having admired this tremendous natural phenomenon and sacrificed countless megapixels to it return to the junction. Here turn left, still on the PR-CV 151 to the Penya Escoda. The track contours round the head of the valley and past a house where you can try to pick out the arches against the surrounding cliffs. At the next junction take the left hand path for the third of the diversions, this time to the **Penya Escoda** as far as an information board with fine views over the valley and down towards Castell de Castells.

Walker dwarfed by the gaping mouth of Els Arcs (photo: Christine Kennett)

147

From here retrace your steps to the junction and turn left to Plan d'Aialt. At a junction, just beyond a house turn left on a broad grass track between almond groves. At the road turn right for the 100 metres or so and then turn left to arrive back at the car.

WALK 33

Embassament de Guadalest

Start/finish	Dam of Guadalest Reservoir
Distance	10km
Grade	Easy
Time	3hrs
Terrain	Metalled roads and good tracks
Height gain	Negligible
Map	Serra d'Aitana (Terra Firma)/Costa Blanca Mountains (Discovery)
Access	The walk starts from the dam, which is reached by a side road off the CV 755 from Collosa d'En Sarria, 1.5km from Guadalest.
Parking	By the dam.

As an easy circuit of one of the few extensive sheets of water in a porous limestone landscape this short, almost level, walk is in sharp contrast to ascents of the high ridges and peaks that surround it, especially the Serrella. Taking three hours or less to complete, it is ideal for a rest day or combined with a visit to Guadalest. The village, with its castle perched high on a cliff, is one of the most popular in the area, its status summed up in a single statistic: each year its 200 inhabitants welcome more than a million tourists. Fortunately most of those visitors cram themselves into the narrow streets and souvenir shops around the castle leaving this gentle scenic walk free for others to enjoy in peace.

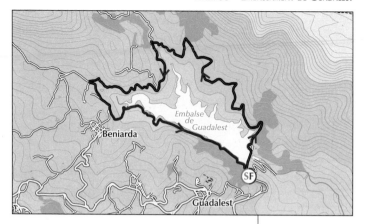

From the parking area cross the dam and take in the excellent views up the lake to the surrounding summits but do not expect to have this first section to yourself. It is popular with joggers, grandmothers with toddlers, dog walkers and couples working up an appetite for lunch in one of the many restaurants.

Guadalest perched on its cliffs

As you carry on along the road the other walkers thin out and soon you should be enjoying the walk in near solitude. Although tarmacked the road is officially classified as a Camino Rural, meaning you are likely to meet little or no traffic. Carry on along the road, ignoring various paths that seem to lead down to the water's edge. ◀

The easy going underfoot makes it all the simpler to admire the dramatic rock scenery on all sides.

After 4km the road comes to a junction with a footpath sign pointing down the road branching off rightwards to Cumbre Aixorta. Instead take the left hand fork leading back towards the reservoir with Guadalest perched on its rocky tower in front. After another couple of kilometres the road reaches a small bridge over the Guadalest River, which feeds the reservoir.

Cross over and take the road climbing leftwards towards the village of **Beniarda**. It passes a small pool and then the much larger municipal swimming pool. The road turns a right hand bend and just as it is about to enter the village take the tarmac track heading down leftwards to the waterside. At the bottom of the hill keep right into a flat area, which is left by a path at its far end. The path crosses a small stream via stepping stones before passing under power lines and then turning to follow the bank of the reservoir. The power lines will be constant companions all the way back to the dam but the high mountains of the Serrella on the other side of the lake prove more than an ample distraction.

WALK 34

Aitana

Start/finish	Font de Partagat, near Benifato
Distance	10km
Grade	Moderate plus a short scramble
Time	4hrs
Terrain	Unmade roads, steep narrow paths and a brief scramble
Height gain	550m
Map	Serra d'Aitana (Terra Firma)/Costa Blanca Mountains (Discovery)
Access	From Collosa d'En Sarria or Polop continue up the CV 70 past Guadalest and Benimantell and take the left turn into Benifato. After 300 metres look out for a small junction on the right with a ceramic plaque on the wall reading Font de Partagat. Take this road and follow it for 4km as it climbs to the large picnic area at the font.
Parking	By the font.
Note	The short scramble through the Passet de la Rabosa demands a little agility and the descent from the passet is over loose scree which requires care.

Viewed from afar Aitana is a bit boring. Despite being the highest mountain in Alicante Province it commands little respect, compared to its junior neighbour, the slightly lower but infinitely more charismatic Puig Campana. Aitana's slightly lumpen, rather nondescript ridge can be hard to pick out in distant views and often demands the sight of the radome on the summit to confirm its identity. So it is a pleasant surprise to discover on closer acquaintance that Aitana has no shortage of character and even boasts a very memorable secret door.

This walk could also easily be combined with the Penya Mulero (Walk 35) to give a longer traverse of the ridge but one of the walks would have to be done in reverse.

From the Font de Partegat take the wide dirt road which climbs up the slope to the left. Ignore the first junction to the left and a few paces higher up at a signpost take the left fork. This is the path to the Collado de Tagarina also used during the ascent of Penya Mulero (Walk 35). At the **Collado de Tagarina** turn right and climb the vegetated slope via a now slightly narrower path. As it gains height it becomes progressively rougher and in places is hard to follow but essentially stays close to the escarpment overlooking the Guadalest Valley. The views in all directions are spectacular and extensive, giving plenty of excuse for stops as this is the sort of ground where it is necessary to watch your feet while actually moving. The main path bypasses the subsidiary summit of the **Pena Alta** and drops to a col before another slight rise.

As you breast this final rise the atmosphere of the mountain changes and you are confronted by the remains of a huge landslip which has left deep chasms in the opposite slope where part of the escarpment has fallen away. ◄

This is a good vantage point from which to get your bearings: the left hand cleft is key to the Passet de la Rabosa, better known to British walkers as Fat Man's Agony.

Now for the summit of **Aitana**. The path climbs steadily to the top even though it is impossible to stand on the highest point, which is safely tucked away behind the military's razor wire amid a forest of aerials and domes.

The radomes that crown Aitana, Alicante's highest peak

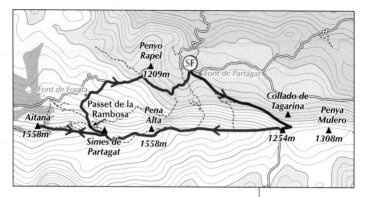

Modern generals, it seems, are just as fond of **summits** as their castle-building medieval forbears. None of this ironmongery has done anything to enhance the beauty of the top but the views in all directions from Valencia in the north down to Murcia in the south and an endless procession of peaks offer full compensation.

Having taken your fill of the view retrace your steps to the col; omitting this leg would save you 45mins.

Now it is time to turn your attention to the surprise package. A wooden sign points to the **Passet de la Rabosa** and it is most easily reached by taking a faint path up the right hand flank of the left hand chasm almost directly in line with a small window in the ridge ahead. The way seems blocked by a huge square boulder but at the last moment a route – Fat Man's Agony – appears.

The landslip has left a secret passageway through the cliffs that guard the steep face of Aitana. At first it seems there is no way through the jumbled blocks which obstruct the exit from the cleft but a couple of yellow and white paint flashes mark the narrowest of gaps between the rocks. The squeeze is indeed no place for a Fat Man nor, come to that, a thin one with a rucksack. A 42in chest seems to be about the maximum that will fit

The tight squeeze of Fat Man's Agony

through upright. Those of more ample girth will have to crawl through the wider gap at the bottom.

Once through this, a second, slightly wider cleft must be descended by a couple of scrambling moves, which are still quite constricted. A steep and slightly unstable path then leads down a jumble of blocks to a path. A few rudimentary wooden steps make things slightly easier.

At the bottom three paths head off across the hillside, a faint upper one, a wide lower one and the middle one of springy earth. Take this as it contours across the hillside, passing wooden signs and information boards describing the native plants. In about 10mins the path reaches the **Font de Forata** and a series of linked descending channels.

Below the font turn right along the broad track signed to Benifato, passing a *nevera* (snow pit) on the left. At the first fork carry on straight ahead slightly downhill. At the next junction ignore the left turn and again carry on straight ahead. Soon the track narrows to become a path and descends steeply through thorn bushes to another spring, the Font de Mandas. From here the path drops steeply again, surprisingly muddy in places, before starting a long rightward traverse across the slope. Eventually it emerges on a wider track by a signpost. Turn left downhill, following more yellow and white flashes, to the car park.

WALK 35
Penya Mulero

Start/finish	Font del Moli, near Guadalest
Distance	11km
Grade	Moderate
Time	3 to 4hrs
Terrain	Unmade roads and narrow tracks
Height gain	575m
Map	Serra d'Aitana (Terra Firma)/Costa Blanca Mountains (Discovery)
Access	The walk starts from the car park at the Font del Moli picnic area, which is reached from the CV 70 Polop to Guadalest road. Turn off this uphill at Km 33.7 by a sign to the Restaurant El Trestellador. At a junction shortly after leaving the CV 70 go right and 1.3km from the CV 70 leave your car in the picnic area car park by a group of houses on the left of the road.

The Penya Mulero is a continuation of the great ridge of Aitana, Alicante's highest peak, and its position makes it an exceptional viewpoint from which to admire the surrounding tops and the Guadalest Valley. For once the going underfoot is mostly easy on wide unmade roads and tracks, allowing plenty of opportunities to admire the views. It is especially lovely in February and early March when the almond trees are covered in pink and white blossom.

This walk passes close to the Font de Partagat, the start point for the ascent of Aitana (Walk 34), so the two can be easily combined to give a full day's expedition.

From the parking area take the chained road running up to the left of the picnic area to reach the font itself where the water emerges from the mouth of a carved lion. Take the steep path up the slope to the left of the font to reach a broad unmade road. Turn right up this and carry on round a right hand hairpin by a dirt parking area, continuing to climb. Ignore a road heading straight ahead on the next bend, marked by a dead end sign. A few paces further up the hill another broad road heads off rightwards through the almond groves. Take this. The road continuing uphill is our return route. Within a few minutes the road passes a deep nevera (snow pit) on the right before entering an area of rock pinnacles and, climbing through a rocky gateway and on past a *finca*, the **Corral de Senyores**. It continues to climb to a col and as it reaches the top the masts on top of Aitana come into view. When it reaches a T-junction turn right and continue across the slope. As you wander along this easy track there is ample opportunity to admire the cliffs of Aitana up ahead and the ridges of the Serrella away to the right. After 15mins the path comes to a T-junction on the brink of a deep ravine. ◀

Below is the parking area of the Font de Partagat, starting point of the Ascent of Aitana (Walk 34) should you wish to link the two.

From the junction turn left uphill and at the fork a few metres higher take the left hand branch and follow the broad track as it rises leftwards across the slope. This is the start of a 30min climb.

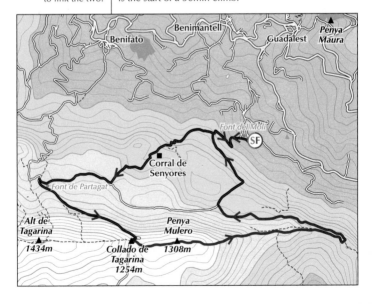

156

After a final step pull and a hairpin bend the path arrives on the broad ridge. Turn left to climb the slopes of the Penyo. ▶ The summit of **Penya Mulero**, reached in about another 15mins, is a magnificent 360 degree viewpoint with the highest mountains of the Costa Blanca at hand while the coast stretches away northwards to Valencia and south to Alicante.

Leaving the summit the track, which so far has been vehicle width, now becomes single track as it weaves through undergrowth and scrub to descend the other side of the ridge. At the bottom of the slope, about 15mins from the summit, the path reaches a pair of small cairns marking a rocky cleft angling back leftwards towards the Guadalest Valley. Drop down this through bushes and across a scree slope to join an almond terrace, still descending leftwards.

When it reaches a junction of tracks head half left down the broad track, which curls back round rightwards and is followed to the junction taken on the outward leg. Carry on down the approach track which can be followed all the way to the car park without the need to use the steep ascent path.

Penya Mulero

To the right the Puig, second highest mountain in the province, seems almost close enough to touch, with the Ponoig and Xanchet even closer.

WALK 36

Alt de la Penya de Sella

Start/finish	Font Pouet Alemany, above Sella
Distance	6km
Grade	Easy
Time	2hrs
Terrain	Forest tracks and a high open ridge
Height gain	250m
Map	Serra d'Aitana (Terra Firma)/Costa Blanca Mountains (Discovery)
Access	From Sella take the CV 770 north for about 5km and 200 metres beyond the 20km marker turn right on a sharp left hand bend to take a tarmac road heading into the valley. Follow this for another 7km to its end at the Font Pouet Alemany.
Parking	Roadside parking by the font.

The Costa Blanca Mountains are blessed with many small roads that stretch deep into the hills and valleys and occasionally that means walkers can enjoy the highest ridges with minimal effort. The Penya de Sella is a magnificent ridge that can be reached by an arduous grind up a scree slope from the picturesque village of Sella but this route sneaks behind the mountain's defences to approach from the Val de Tagarina on the opposite side of the range and lets horse power do the hard work. It is a short walk with rewards far beyond the effort required and ideal for a short day or combined with sightseeing or relaxing in Sella and Finestrat.

From the parking area take the rightward slanting track that climbs the hill. Ignore the first track to the left, which leads to a ruin, and take the second one a few metres further on and marked with a cairn and a blue paint spot. It passes another house until at the top of the cultivated terraces the track becomes a narrow path. Follow this uphill for about 20 metres and then take the path on the right, which climbs up through the trees to another terrace

on the left. Go along this almost to its end to where an unmarked path climbs to the col through a band of gorse, which may embarrass those wearing shorts.

> The arrival at the ridge is rewarded with fabulous **views** down to the Castellet Ridge guarding the huge bulk of the Puig Campana behind. To the left the sharp peak of the Divino dominates while to the right our ridge stretches invitingly away. The ridge of Aitana, Alicante's highest peak, crowned with its golf ball radome, completes the view. It is almost astonishing that such a majestic view can be had for such trivial effort.

Sella and the Puig

Head right, the start of a delightful switchback, to climb the open slope of broken limestone. Drop down to a second col and then climb to the summit of the **Alt de la Penya de Sella** itself before picking your way down the limestone slabs to a third col where the ridge route meets the path coming up from Sella and yellow and white markers appear. ◄

The next rise is crowned by a circular hollow cairn, while at the far end of the ridge the restored Mas de Dalt sits surreally above the cliffs. It is possible to extend the pleasure by walking along to that. From the circular cairn continue along the ridge for 50 metres to a junction with a path hooking back rightwards. This drops through trees and terraces to become an easy track descending diagonally across the hillside to reach the car park in less than half an hour and the end of a surprising stroll.

The route from Sella, although on a PR-CV, is hideous, involving a long, joyless slog up scree to a cave before an equally unpleasant slither back to the village.

WALK 37
Barranc de l'Arc and Barranc del Xarquer

Start/finish	Refugio de l'Arc, near Sella
Distance	12km
Grade	Moderate
Time	3 to 4hrs
Terrain	Forestry roads and clear paths
Height gain	320m
Map	Serra d'Aitana (Terra Firma)/Costa Blanca Mountains (Discovery)
Access	Approach Sella from the coast on the CV 770. Cross the bridge over the Riu Sella and then drive uphill towards the town. At a sharp left bend turn right following signs for the cemetery. At the next T-junction turn right and follow the road for about 3.8km to where the tarmac ends at a fork. Turn right down a forestry road for a few metres and park by the climbers' refuge.

Sella sits among some of the finest mountain scenery in the area but, even here, not every summit needs to be climbed to appreciate the splendour of its setting. In some cases, as in Walk 36 it is possible to drive almost to the top of the mountains. This fairly gentle excursion manages to enjoy some of the finest rock scenery on offer in two neighbouring valleys without the need to expend very much effort at all.

From the refuge go back to the fork in the road and take the forestry road heading straight up the valley and signed PR-CV 9 to Benimaurell. This will be our route all the way to the head of the valley. Directly in front is the great pointed summit of the Divino, one of the great rock faces of the Costa Blanca

> Divino attracts climbers from all over the world to scale the huge wall. On the opposite side of the valley is what looks like a massive tombstone-shaped flake which seems to be slowly peeling away from the mountain.

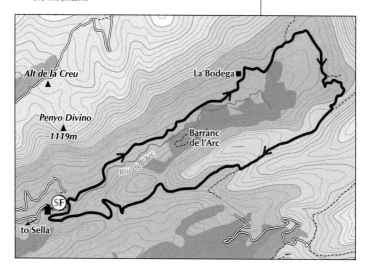

The road climbs easily through cultivated terraces, passing occasional houses in various states of disrepair and renovation while at the head of the valley sits the Pena Roc, flanked by the switchback path of the Paso de los Contadores.

The road passes **La Bodega** and then comes to two forks in quick succession. In both cases stay on the main track. At the first go right and at the second go left. After an hour or so of steady walking from the refuge the road begins to curl round the head of the valley and meets another fork. The left hand option climbs up to the paso but we gratefully ignore this and carry on straight ahead on the level track as it crosses the head of the valley offering excellent views down between the towering orange and grey walls towards Sella.

However, we cannot reach the second valley, the Barranc del Xarquer, without at least some climbing and soon the road comes to another house on the right. A couple of hundred metres beyond this, where the road turns sharp left, we leave it to take a narrower path climbing off to the right up the valley side. Soon it

The broad valley of the Barranc de l'Arc

reaches a ruined house which it squeezes behind and then continues, now rockier and rougher, up the edge of the barranc, passing a small spring and water trough before emerging in an area of terraces grazed by horses. It continues up through the terraces and meets a broader track. Turn right along this as it makes its way up to the col. The path soon crosses the watershed with a minimum of fuss. There is no great crossroads here and it simply dives into the next valley. ▸

Having got your breath back carry on down the narrow path as it works its way through some occasionally aggressive undergrowth and trees. After about 15mins it arrives at cultivated terraces and a painted rock lying on the ground with a three way sign on it. Turn right towards the houses signed towards Sella. Cross the terrace and climb the opposite side, still following signs to Sella. Cross a dirt road and carry on climbing towards an orange-painted house. Just before you reach it turn left by another house with a row of cypress trees beside it and take the road past it heading gently downhill. After 100 metres or so at a three-way junction carry on straight ahead, still going downhill while across the valley the huge presence of the Puig Campana and the more delicate tracery of the jagged Castellet Ridge command attention.

The track slowly descends this exquisite valley making for the dip in the ridge through which you can see Sella. Ignore a track rising off to the right and stay on the main road as it eventually curves beneath a rock face studded with climbing bolts – and often a Babel of multinational climbers enjoying themselves on the routes.

At a T-junction turn right and follow the forest road back to the car park at the end of a satisfying half day that will have filled you with pleasure without taking very much out of you.

It is worth taking a little breather here to admire the change in scenery and the sight of Sella, neatly framed by a gap in the ridge to the right.

WALK 38

Tour of Xanchet

Start/finish	Parking area at the top of the concrete road in the Vall de Guadar (near Polop)
Distance	14km
Grade	Moderate
Time	4hrs
Terrain	Broad tracks and level paths
Height gain	620m
Map	Serra d'Aitana (Terra Firma)/Costa Blanca Mountains (Discovery)
Access	From the coast take the CV 70 to Polop and then take the ring road signed to Guadalest. At the fifth roundabout, planted with olive trees and signed 'Cami', turn left and follow the road steeply uphill below climbers' crags to a large parking area at the top of the surfaced road.

Perhaps some mountains are just not meant to be climbed. Xanchet or Sanchet, which towers over the picturesque town of Polop, appears to be one of them. Amazingly for such a prominent and attractive summit, and unlike its neighbours, the Ponoig and the Puig Campana, there is no clearly defined path to the top. Instead it has this exquisite *volta* (circuit), which completely encircles it and offers constantly changing views from delightful paths. Determined peak baggers will find it possible to pick a way to the top up shifting scree, small outcrops and sharp rocks with the occasional cairn to mark the way but devotees of the volta would tell you that incorporating such an unpleasant scrabble into what is a near perfect circuit would be, like the proverbial round of golf, a good walk ruined. Perhaps one day the path builders will give the mountain the summit path its status deserves but until then enjoy this delectable round, often said to be best walk in the area.

The Vall de Guadar is also known to climbers as Echo Valley.

From the parking area set off along the dirt track continuation of the concrete road surrounded on all sides by huge rock faces. ◀ After a series of bends it reaches the blue-painted Casa de Deu which stands on a junction of

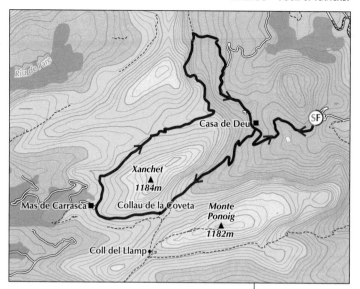

tracks. Take the PR-CV 17 signed to the Coll dell Llamp 1hr 20 mins away. This is the beginning of the circuit. Eventually the path becomes narrower as it makes its way up the valley towards the col and passing below vast walls of orange and grey limestone. At the next signpost at the **Collau de la Coveta de la Moscada** reached by about an hour's steady ascent from the car take an unsigned path breaking off to the right and marked with green paint. It climbs to a shallow col a few metres higher and is the same path taken during the descent from the Ponoig (Walk 39).

At a fork after a couple of hundred metres go right on a clear path, passing a cairn with a yellow and white cross on it. Ignore this sign, which is for walkers on the separate PR-CV, which heads down the valley, and warns that they are straying from their route. It is, however, our course so continue on the path through the woods circling round the mountain. It is marked by the occasional cairn as it weaves through the pines and rocky outcrops.

Path to the Collau de la Coveta

The path steers a fairly level course and emerges on an open slope with the jagged ridge of the Castellets filling the foreground. Along this section purple paint appears to mark the way but the path is clear enough, including occasional sections of easy scrambling. Half an hour's steady traversing brings you to the substantial and unmistakeable **Mas de Carrasca**, its name emblazoned in huge letters over the door.

From here contour round the terraces, which run around the bowl behind the house. The path descends a short way and after about 200 metres it forks. Take the right hand option, maintaining height. It surmounts a small rock band and then crosses a low col. As the path contours round the right hand side of the valley the views change yet again. ◄

Wide open panoramas of earlier sections are now replaced by a more intimate little valley with the high ridges of Xanchet above.

Once across the next small col the path becomes enclosed by pines again with only occasional glimpses of the surrounding crags and another substantial house, the Mas de Papatxi, across the valley. As the path comes into open ground by the Mas hook back sharply right on a path clinging to the right hand side of the valley now with the ridges of the Bernia and Ferrer in front. The path passes between rocks, now with fine open views across the woods and terraces of the valley to Callosa d'En Sarria. Continue downwards before the path heads off a disconcertingly long way leftwards under a huge scooped out orange wall and then on beneath towering spires of limestone. ▸

As the path descends look for a narrow path off to the right, marked with red paint and a small cairn, which angles down the slope. It emerges on a hairpin bend on an unmade road. Take the left hand fork downhill. It soon becomes concreted and joins another road by three stunted stone pillars. Take the right hand option and begin climbing slowly uphill. The road becomes unsurfaced and when it reaches a junction carry on straight ahead to reach the blue **Casa de Deu** and complete the volta. All that remains is to drop down the road back to the car following the PR-CV 17 signed to Polop.

As you finally begin to lose height the reason for the diversion becomes apparent as a backward glance reveals huge precipices in the area below the path.

WALK 39
Monte Ponoig

Start/finish	Roadhead 4.5km beyond the Font del Moli, near Finestrat
Distance	12km
Grade	Moderate
Time	4 to 5hrs
Terrain	Forest tracks, narrow paths and a short scramble
Height gain	640m
Map	Serra d'Aitana (Terra Firma)/Costa Blanca Mountains (Discovery)
Access	From Finestrat take the narrow uphill road signed to the Font del Moli. Carry on past the font and on up the road for 3.5km to a T-junction. Turn right and 100 metres further on turn right again to where the tarmac ends after 1km.
Parking	Unmade car park.

The Ponoig offers a fine isolated summit and this route reaches it by a splendid day's walking in the company of some of the Costa Blanca's highest summits with a classic mixture of steep tracks and dense woodland followed by an airy scramble. It ends with an easy descent to the valley using mostly unmade roads before a final flourish crossing below a magnificent crenelated ridge decorated with enough towers and pinnacles to quicken the pulse of any mountaineer.

Path to the Coll de Llamp

Walk up the forest road continuation of the tarmac for a few paces and then take a track marked by a small red arrow on the right and climbing the hill before starting to traverse towards the col at the head of the valley, your first objective. At a fork go right continuing across the valley side. When it meets another broad track on a bend take the uphill option still heading towards the col. In less than 5mins it arrives at a prominent cairn marking a clear path heading uphill and signed with red dots and a large green arrow. Turn up this until after 15mins steady climbing the reason for the elaborate cairning is revealed when

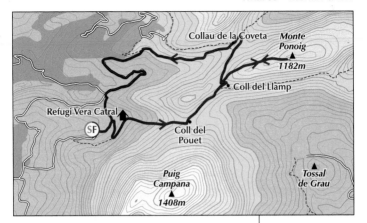

the path reaches the **Refugi Vera Catral**. ▸ You are now briefly joining the Volta del Puig Campana (Walk 40).

From the refuge take the upper path behind it marked by yellow and white paint, which becomes a broad forestry road. In less than 15mins you arrive at the **Coll del Pouet**, where paths seem to arrive from all directions. Turn left along the PR-CV 13 to Polop, still following yellow and white markers (although be wary, there is yellow and white paint on almost every path).

As you leave the confines of the valley the views to the coast open up. The path crosses the slopes and climbs past small pinnacles to the **Coll del Llamp**, which makes a good spot for a breather before tackling the final 2km climb to the summit of **Monte Ponoig**. There is a choice of routes to take. For those with a head for heights an airy scramble rightwards follows the crest while an easier, less exposed path climbs below the lefthand side of the ridge.

The **summit** is a surprisingly grassy area with a book to be signed by all who reach the top. A glance through the pages is testament to the international pull of these mountains with an astonishing range of nationalities represented.

A less-than-homely tin shack with little to commend it except its magnificent location, but popular with climbers visiting the local crags.

The Ponoig summit book signed by walkers from all over the world

After enjoying the 360 degree panorama return to the Coll del Llamp and then turn downhill rightwards, once again following the yellow and white markers. Here the character of the walk changes again. After having extensive views of the coastal developments, notably Benidorm, on the climb from the Pouet you are now back in wild mountain country dominated by the massive rock walls of Xanchet and the jagged chain of the Castellets with the horizon crowded by summits and ridges.

Following the path downwards you seem to heading to the wrong valley but it curls round a rocky knoll to reach a signpost by the **Collau de la Coveta de la Moscada**, 700 metres from the Collau del Llamp. Here ignore the signed paths and instead take an unmarked path leftwards up a clear path over a shallow col a few metres higher up where the yellow and white waymarks reappear. After about 100 metres a very clear path heads rightwards into the trees. Ignore this. It is part of the popular Xanchet circuit (Walk 38). Instead carry on down the valley following yellow and white flashes.

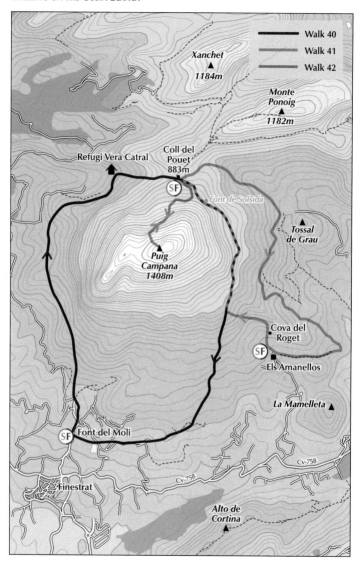

PUIG CAMPANA

Viewed from Finestrat the Puig Campana (pronounce it Putch) is every child's idea of what a mountain ought to look like. Its triangular profile ends in a sharply pointed summit with near vertical flanks girdled by impossible-looking rock faces. Seen from Benidorm it is the most easily identified mountain on the coast, thanks to Rondal's Notch, a square cut bite taken from its summit ridge. Although only the second highest peak in Alicante province and a full 150m lower than Aitana it dominates every view in which it appears and draws the eye from all directions. Anything the Puig lacks in altitude it more than makes up for in attitude with a wild majesty that fires the imagination, quickens the pulse and dares you to try to climb it.

WALK 40
Volta del Puig Campana

Start/finish	Font del Moli, Finestrat
Distance	11km
Grade	Moderate
Time	3 to 4hrs
Terrain	Mountain paths, some steep and eroded
Height gain	600m
Map	Serra d'Aitana (Terra Firma)/Costa Blanca Mountains (Discovery)
Access	From Finestrat take the narrow uphill road signed 'Font del Moli' and park in the large car park at the font.

This is the classic round of the Puig and offers constantly changing views as it encircles this iconic peak. It also offers grandstand views of the imposing rock architecture of the jagged Castellets Ridge as well as the formidable faces of the adjoining Ponoig and Xanchet. It follows the PR-CV 289 and is well waymarked throughout. Despite the spectacular terrain through which it passes, it is friendly walking with no nasty surprises.

The spartan Vera Catral climbers' refuge

The metal exterior and steel bunks of this climbers' hut built in 1979 do not make it the most enticing spot to stay but there's no denying the appeal of its position.

From the car park walk up the road and round a left hand bend and then take a track up through the woods to rejoin the road at a bridge. Immediately across this take a track branching up to the right and another smaller parking area. After a few paces take a path the left signed 'Coll del Pouet PR-CV 289'. The path climbs through pines and views in the clearings are of the coast until the track curls round the mountain to a more open area to reveal the golf ball radome on top of Aitana, the only mountain in the Alicante Province to top the Puig. A little over an hour's hard climbing interspersed with occasional flatter sections to regain your breath brings you to the spartan hovel of the **Refugio Vera Catral**. ◄

From the refuge take the higher of two paths climbing away up leftwards behind it and marked by white and yellow paint. This quickly leads to a broader track that goes on to the **Coll del Pouet**, a meeting place for many tracks and a handy place for a refreshment stop. Above are the towering faces of the Ponoig. Leave it by a rising track to the right marked Font de Moli per Foia Cac PR-CV 289 and Font de Solsida and a more rustic sign reading Sender Botanic to L'Ombria del Puig Campana, which climbs the hillside. Within a couple of hundred metres you come to a junction on a hairpin bend. The path signed to the summit (Walk 42) sets off up the hillside on a broad track while the continuation of the volta heads back to **Font del Moli**.

The path initially climbs and then levels out to begin the second half of the circuit of the mountain. This section was devastated by fire in 2009 and, although the area is slowly recovering, its extent is yet another reminder of the need to take care not to start fires, particularly with carelessly discarded cigarettes, in this arid landscape.

After 400 metres the path passes the now-dry Font de la Solsida at the foot of a sheer limestone face. After such a wild mountain interlude it is slightly surreal to turn the next corner and see the Manhattanesque skyline of Benidorm ahead. The path continues across rock ledges marked by yellow and white paint and carries on across a broad barranc to continue round the mountain until the distinctive landmark of Rondal's Notch comes into view. It drops into another barranc and climbs out to enter a stretch of pine woodland. At an unsurfaced road with a fine view of the Puig to the right carry on straight ahead into the woods until the path emerges onto a tarmacked road. Turn right along this and continue when it becomes unsurfaced. At a T-junction turn left to cross a bridge and carry on downhill to the car park.

Nearing the end of the Volta

WALK 41
Coll del Pouet

Start/finish	Els Amanellos below Cova del Roget
Distance	10km
Grade	Moderate
Time	3hrs
Terrain	Good paths and tracks, steep climbs
Height gain	590m
Map	Serra d'Aitana (Terra Firma)/Costa Blanca Mountains (Discovery)
Access	From the N332 take the CV 70 and turn off onto the CV 758 towards Finestrat. After 4.5km turn right opposite the El Pages restaurant following signs to the Shieldaig Kennels. After another kilometre fork left and after another kilometre where the tarmac ends park on rough ground by a yellow and white house.

This walk makes use of a section of the popular volta which encircles the Puig Campana but rather than continuing round the mountain it explores the eastern slopes and barrancs. Because it starts higher up the mountain it also feels slightly easier as an approach to the Coll del Pouet and the 1408m summit of the Puig. Like the volta, it gives close up views of the huge faces of the Ponoig, Xanchet and the Puig itself.

Walk up the broad track beside the house for a few metres towards the large **Cova del Roget** above but after a few steps take a narrow path on the left marked by a substantial cairn. The path begins to climb steeply and when you come to a T-junction turn left through the pines and after about 5mins it comes to a large pine growing in the centre of the track. Just beyond this turn right up a path with a veritable rainbow of paint marks, including yellow and white flashes. Head up the hill with the square cut of Rondal's Notch directly above. After a couple minutes

Start of the climb to the Coll de Pouet

go left at a fork sticking with the broader path. In another 15mins the path reaches a T-junction with a broader path. Turn right up this. ▶

The first section is 30mins of steep climbing to reach a signpost pointing the way to the Coll del Pouet. The path now levels a little and begins to traverse across the mountain with tall crags above and the towers of Benidorm below, while the Penon at Calp and the Bernia come into view ahead, soon joined by the Ponoig. After another 30mins of steady walking the path reaches the Font de Solsida. Carry on towards the Coll del Pouet, 600 metres further on. ▶

Along the way the path passes the signposted track leading to the summit of the Puig another 4.3km away (see Walk 42). In another 200 metres the path reaches the **Coll del Pouet**, the spaghetti junction of the range with paths and people emerging and disappearing in all directions. It is also a popular, if somewhat busy spot for refreshments with a handy dinner tabled-sized rock. However, a quieter option awaits us a little further down the mountain.

This is part of the volta, the main circuit of the Puig, but you will most likely find yourself walking against the main flow of hikers, as most walk it in a clockwise direction.

Away to the right the scene is dominated by the faces of the Ponoig and, looking through the dip of the Collau del Llamp, the enormous cliffs of Xanchet.

Set off down the broad PR-CV 17 signed to Polop Tarbena Margoig. Continue down the track for 20mins or so to reach a fenced off picnic area by a restored lime kiln, which makes a handy refreshment stop. From here continue down the track for another 5mins to reach a bend by a farmhouse where two tracks head off rightwards. Take the second, smaller path that curls down a barranc with small cliffs while to the front the Serra Gelada and later Benidorm appear. Follow the path to a junction and there take the left hand path which heads over a small crest and follow it down the ridge to a shallow col guarded by a large pine. Take a path heading rightwards down into a barranc before climbing steeply up the opposite slope where it curves round the head of a gully. Ignore all side tracks until it comes to a fork. Go right on a path that curls round the shoulder of a hill to reach a broad track above a ruin. Here turn left and then almost immediately right opposite the ruin on a path that aims for a col marked by a power pylon. Just beyond the pylon take a track on the right and follow it back to **Els Amanellos**.

WALK 42

Puig Campana Summit from the Coll del Pouet

Start/finish	Coll del Pouet
Distance	4.6km (plus whichever approach you choose)
Grade	Strenuous
Time	2hrs 30mins to 3hrs (plus time for ascent and descent to and from the Coll del Pouet)
Terrain	Steep mountain paths
Height gain	625m
Map	Serra d'Aitana (Terra Firma)/Costa Blanca Mountains (Discovery)
Access	On foot from the start points of Walks 39 (2km, 30mins), 40 (5kms, 1hr 30mins) or 41 (3.5km, 1hr)
Parking	None.

It is possible to climb the Puig as a complete traverse, ascending an all-too-obvious gully up the south face and dropping down a well-worn path northwards to the Coll del Pouet. The gully, however, is a worn mess of scree fit only for masochists and would-be SAS types. It provides a joyless trudge going up and a precarious slither coming down and is best avoided in either direction. Instead this route climbs up the northern slopes to reach the 1408m peak and returns the same way. It means covering the same ground in ascent and descent but the Puig deserves to be enjoyed, not endured.

For those seeking the shortest and easiest way to the summit and who do not mind following the same route throughout it is possible to follow the start of the Ponoig route (Walk 39) as far as the Coll del Pouet and then reverse it in the descent.

From the Coll del Pouet take the PR-CV 289 which rises south eastwards up the flank of the Puig, signed 'Font de Moli per Foia Cac PR-CV 289 and Font de Solsida' and a more rustic signed reading Sender Botanic to L'Ombria del Puig Campana, which climbs the hillside. Within a couple of hundred metres you come to a junction on a hairpin bend. The path signed to the summit (Cim) sets

The enticing rocky summit of the Puig

off uphill on a broad track. Take this and where the broad track becomes a narrower path carry on and at a junction of paths go right to continue climbing, picking your way through bands of rock and scree and following blue and green paint marks. After an hour or so of unremitting ascent the path reaches a col and views open up to the coast. This col is also the top of the ascent of the gully from Finestrat. Turn left up the broken slope. The path breaks down into any number of variations but probably the easiest to follow is one marked with blue and red paint that moves round to the slope overlooking Benidorm and a deceptively insignificant-looking Serra Gelada far below. The top of **Puig Campana** is reached in about 20 mins from the col.

> The **summit** is a superb viewpoint with a 360 degree panorama from the north coast and Penon de Ifach round to the Bernia, the neighbouring peaks of the Ponoig, Xanchet and Aitana then back round to the coast down to Alicante and Murcia, while at your feet are the Sierra Cortina and Benidorm.

The descent route reverses the climb to the col and then down the ascent path towards the **Coll del Pouet**.

THE SERRELLA

Soaring cliffs of the Barranc de la Canal (Walk 44)

CAUTION

It is fair to say that walking in the Serrella is often in a league of its own, and not only because its peaks are so magnificent. Expeditions here demand a greater degree of self-sufficiency than is usually called for in the rest of the Costa Blanca, including an ability sometimes to pick your own way through difficult terrain. Waymarking is often non-existent and most paths receive scant, if any, maintenance, while the kilometres can feel particularly long. For confident and experienced mountaineers there is no better walking to be had in this part of Spain but the less experienced may feel rather out on a limb.

WALK 43

Penya del Castellet

Start/finish	Castellet recreation area above Castell de Castells
Distance	11.5km
Grade	Moderate
Time	3 to 4hrs (plus time to explore the castle)
Terrain	Forest roads, mountain paths and a little easy scrambling
Height gain	430m
Map	Serra d'Aitana (Terra Firma)/Costa Blanca Mountains (Discovery)/La Serrella (El Tossal)
Access	From Collosa d'En Sarria take the C-3318/CV 715 towards Tarbena. Immediately after passing Tarbena take the CV 752 to Castell de Castells. A few hundred metres before reaching the village look out for a sign on the left marked 'El Castellet'. Go up the narrow road and at a fork go left which leads to a parking area, refuge and campsite. Alternatively approach Castells via the Vall de Pop from Xalo.

The 'castellet' above Castell de Castells has quite a billing to live up to – the Castle of Castles – and it does not disappoint. It is magnificently sited on the very summit of the peak, adding man-made ramparts to already formidable natural defences. The panorama from the top is unsurpassed and it gives a particularly good view of the Barranc de la Canal on the neighbouring Mallada de Llop.

Leave the parking area following a sign for the PR-CV 149 El Castellet. As you walk up the track, passing woods and olive groves, the Serrella stretch away in a series of inviting rocky peaks but that is not today's objective. At a fork keep left. The path soon becomes single track and heads into a ravine with Castells cupped in the valley below. The path, still carrying traces of steps and cobbling from the days when it was major supply route, weaves easily up the hill. As it breasts the ridge the path meets a dirt road, which will be used on the return leg. Here turn left to curl round a knoll still following the signs for the Castellet. From here the walls of the castle, teetering on the brink of a vertical face are clearly visible on the peak but the track begins to curl away from the summit for half a kilometre until it meets a T-junction

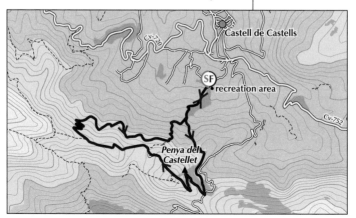

183

Final approach to the castle ruins

As the road curls round below the topmost crags is possible to imagine what a daunting prospect attacking this citadel would have been with assailants at the mercy of defenders on the walls above.

with a concrete road. Turn right up this to quickly reach a crossroads with the PR-CV 18 arriving from Guadalest. Take the right hand arm signed to the Castellet PR-CV 149 and now making for the final tower of the Penya. ◄

The path finally reaches a col and the Mallada del Llop, with the distinctive Barranc de la Canal – 'the Glacier' – scarring its nose leaps into view at the end of the Serrella. The return path goes straight ahead here but first turn from the path to climb the final few metres to the ruins atop **Penya del Castellet**.

The **castle**, with its blend of natural and man-made defences, can still be admired in its ruined state. The 360 degree panorama and the views down to the turquoise water of the Guadalest reservoir in the valley below are stunning. Beyond stand the giants of the Costa Blanca, Aitana, the Puig, the Ponoig and Xanchet. The defenders of this eyrie must have felt themselves invincible and for today's visitors with more peaceful intentions no restaurant terrace has a view to match this perfect refreshment stop.

When you have explored the ruins return to the col and follow the track onward downhill. It reaches a col and then climbs again to a viewpoint overlooking the

Barranc de la Canal. At a small flat area by some corrals it is possible to take a small path to a viewpoint overlooking the Canal but the main track continues downhill in a series of hairpins until it reaches a three-way junction on a bend. Here leave the main track and continue contouring across the hillside of a broad shelf, still following the PR CV 149. This is an effortless promenade with the chance to admire the surrounding peaks and valleys – a rare treat on these hills where so much time is spent watching your feet on rocky paths – as it makes its way across the hillside to reach the junction passed on the ascent. Here take the single track path back downhill signed to the Area Castellet, 20mins away.

WALK 44
Mallada del Llop

Start/finish	Village square, Famorca
Distance	12km
Grade	Moderate
Time	4 to 5hrs
Terrain	Mountain tracks and paths
Height gain	730m
Map	Costa Blanca Mountains (Discovery)/La Serrella (El Tossal)
Access	Reach Castell de Castells either by following the Vall de Pop or through Collosa d'En Sarria then follow signs to Famorca.

La Serrella is a crescent of rock thrusting up more than 1300m above the Guadalest Valley in a steep rocky escarpment but its northern slopes are more amenable. Its most striking feature is the Barranc de la Canal, a broad, parallel-sided valley biting deep into the uppermost slopes of the serra's eastern peak the Mallada del Llop, which rises above the village of Castell de Castells. The ascent, however, begins from Famorca further up the valley.

From the Placa del Font take a concrete road rising to the left. On a left hand bend a path comes down the terraces. Ignore it for the moment; it will be our return route. At the next junction where the road climbs uphill carry on contouring following a dirt road through the terraces. Similarly ignore the next uphill option and soon the path begins climbing diagonally leftwards across the slope. Where the track appears to run out at a flatter area at the top of the cultivated terraces carry on in the same line for a few metres following the rough path, which soon resumes its traversing line across the slope. With little or no waymarking it does require some cunning to pick out this section of the route. The path attacks the slope in a series of zigzags before coming to a barranc. Continue round this and onwards to another as the views begin to open up and constantly improve.

After more than an hour's hard tramping the ridge is reached and the great trench of the Barranc de la Canal appears although at this stage it is possible to appreciate only the opposite wall with the great whaleback of Aitana beyond.

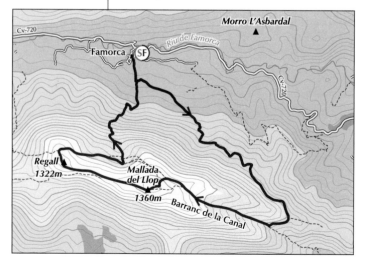

Mallada del Llop with the distinctive Barranc de la Canal

On the ridge is a set of ramshackle corrals built from old fence panels and even bedsteads. Pass to the right of it on a path marked by red paint spots and the occasional cairn. After 10mins or so come to a junction marked by a cairn in a small col below the slopes of a rocky tower blocking the ridge. Turn left still following red dots and cairns to head steeply down into the **Barranc de la Canal** on a zigzag path.

> The **barranc** is wide and rounded but you are hemmed in on both sides by tall rock faces, steep to the north and even steeper to the south. Above is the clear path towards the Mallada del Llop and behind is the Penya del Castellet towering above. Beyond it the ridge fades away towards the sea while in the valley the netting over the vast fruit groves of Callosa stands out clearly.

On the bed of the barranc the path meets one coming up from Guadalest and passes a splendid old snowpit as it climbs to a col before heading diagonally across a slope of fine scree to reach the ridge where, depending on the path

The views stretch
up the coast to
Valencia and beyond
while inland the
mountains of the
Costa Blanca blend
into uncounted serras
stretching away into
the Spanish interior.

you have chosen, it may be necessary to climb back left-wards to reach the 1360m summit of **Mallada del Llop**. ◄

It is possible to make a direct descent to Famorca but after so much effort it is a shame to descend so soon. Instead head west along the ridge making for the next summit, the Regall (1322m) (also called Pico de Serrella) with a rocky turret just below it. After the earlier slow going it is a delight to be able to stride out on a good path with stunning views in every direction. The **Regall**, perched above a vertical escarpment, offers a fine view of the next summit, the Pla de la Casa but there is a deep col between. So instead head downhill northwards towards the col leading to Famorca and passing a lone tree.

At the col turn rightwards downhill along a sketchy path which passes a cairn. The path ignores the first valley heading downhill and contours over another col, passing a limestone pinnacle to your left. At a fork take the lower left hand option, which descends to a font in a locked concrete building. The track joins another coming down from the Mallada.

This path, presumably used by those who maintain the font and the pipe network it feeds, becomes much easier to follow down the bed of the valley. As you step onto the open slopes **Famorca** appears below. Where it reaches a road ignore the tarmac and continue straight downhill on a narrow path, which emerges at the junction passed on the ascent and so back to the village.

A Nativity crib on the summit of the Mallada

WALK 45
Pla de la Casa

Start/finish	Fageca
Distance	13km
Grade	Strenuous
Time	4 to 5hrs
Terrain	Narrow paths, some steep and loose
Height gain	690m
Map	Costa Blanca Mountains (Discovery)/La Serrella (El Tossal)
Access	From Castell de Castells take the CV 720 past Famorca to Fageca.
Parking	Off road by the sports centre on the edge of the village.
Note	The Serrella are among of the wildest mountains on the Costa Blanca and the paths reflect this. Some may find parts of this walk, especially the traverse of the barranc after the Font Roja, a little exciting. A head for heights is required.

The long ridge of the Serrella is a paradise for those who love wild scenery and have a taste for adventure. It also helps if they are not too demanding of fripperies such as waymarking and signposting as on this walk they can be a little haphazard. The reward, however, is magnificent rock scenery and one of the finest summits in the area.

The centre of the village stands above the main road but where the Placa de l'Esglesia drops to meet the CV 720 there is a small area with noticeboards. None of them indicates that the PR-V 182, which makes up much of this walk, starts under the subway beneath the road. Nevertheless go down this and carry on past the **Font de l' Esprite Sant** and an old washhouse and then on along the concrete track following occasional yellow and white paint flashes. At a fork take the right hand branch straight

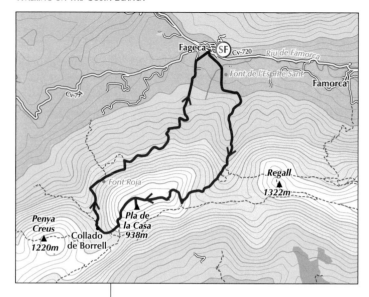

ahead along an unmade road, which climbs through the almond groves. Near the top of the terraces at a junction marked with yellow and white paint turn left on a track along the terraces and after about 100 metres fork right uphill by a cairn.

The path curls round into a barranc with fine cliffs ahead. This is pleasant walking amid interesting rock scenery with a huge walled-in cave in the face away to the right. About an hour's climbing brings you to a walled-in font. Carry on up the remainder of the gorge. Eventually as the path nears the ridge the radome and masts of Aitana come into view across the Guadalest Valley. At a small wooden sign the path turns sharp right heading uphill to a scree fan and a gap in the cliffs above. The path ends at a large shallow bowl with an impressively large snow pit, some 10m deep. The bowl is surrounded by rocky outcrops, any one of which might be the peak from this angle. The way, however, lies leftwards and the path climbs bare rock to the summit.

Ice pit below the summit of Pla de la Casa

And what a **summit**! It stands atop a small semi-detached pinnacle crowned with a metal cross. In all it is scarcely large enough to host a snooker match and requires a brief easy scramble to attain it. Once there you are on the edge of all things, the ground dropping away on all sides but especially dramatically on the southern face overlooking the Guadalest Valley with magnificent far-reaching views. This is truly one of the great panoramas of the Costa Blanca and a stupendous lunch stop.

Summit of the Pla de la Casa

From the summit retrace your steps down to the snow pit. Take the path which skirts its left hand side and follow the track as it runs parallel to the line of the escarpment before diving down a steep eroded gully, which requires considerable care to reach the **Collado de Borrell** where several paths meet from along the ridge and up from the valleys on either side. Here turn right along a narrow trod through the woods following signs for the PRV182 for Fageca.

Soon the path reaches a forest road. Turn down this making for the **Font Roja**, where a sign points down into the barranc. The continuation path can be seen crossing the opposite wall, apparently little more than a faint white line doodled across the slope. Fortunately its bark proves worse than its bite and, while an airy crossing, it is never quite as bad as it looks. Nevertheless a head for heights does come in handy in places. Soon it becomes wider and less exposed as it continues traversing the hillside. At a fork marked with a cairn take the lower left hand option downhill and marked with a post with yellow and white paint a few metres ahead where it begins to drop steeply down the hillside.

> If the path looks too daunting the only alternative is to follow the signed PR-CV 23-24 towards Quatretondeta as far as the Font de l'Espinal (Walk 46). From there, work your way eastwards back to Fageca using the field access roads but this will add 3kms of so to the walk, depending on the route you take.

When it reaches an old font with a long trough turn sharp right following the path which contours across the hillside until, after about 10mins, Fageca comes into view in the valley below. The path carries on traversing, dipping into a series of folds in the hillside before beginning to descend through abandoned terraces and scrub woodland, weaving this way and that but always clear until it drops into a barranc which quickly leads to a tarmac lane heading directly back to **Fageca**.

WALK 46

El Recingle Alt (Pic de Serrella)

Start/finish	Quatretondeta/Cuatretondeta
Distance	13km
Grade	Strenuous
Time	5 to 6hrs
Terrain	Rough mountain paths, steep ascents
Height gain	750m
Map	Costa Blanca Mountains (Discovery)/La Serrella (El Tossal)
Access	From Castell de Castells take the CV 720 to Fageca and then turn onto the CV 754 to Quatretondeta.
Parking	By the bus shelter at the foot of the village.

For those who like wild mountains there is no better range in the whole of the Costa Blanca than the glorious crest of the Serrella, stretching all the way from the Penya del Castellet to the lonely top of the Morro de la Serrella. This walk visits the very roof of the range and ends with a traverse below the fabulous Agulles, an area of superb pinnacles seen at their best in the evening light after a long day on the tops. Some maps give the summit the title of Pic de Serrella but others also award that accolade to El Regall, visited on Walk 44.

From the foot of the village walk 300 metres or so right towards Gorgos and on a bend by a bridge turn left on a concrete road passing the Font del Xorros. Follow the track up past this. At a fork go right and soon reach an asphalt road. Turn left to follow this uphill. After 1.3km from where you joined the road it goes round a double bend. After the left hand of these by a black and white Coto Privado de Caza sign two parallel tracks leave the left hand side of the road. Take the right hand of the two, climbing directly up the hill. (If you reach a stretch of the asphalt road where it starts to descend markedly you have gone too far and missed this turn off).

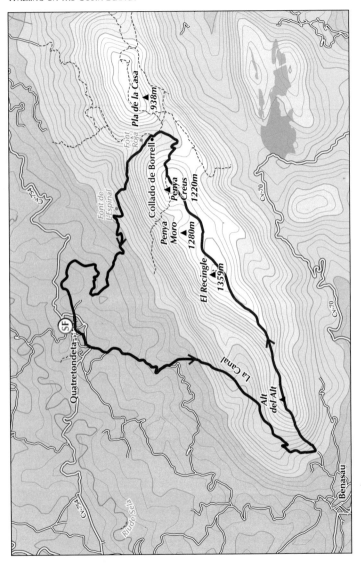

The path arrives at a casita, the Corral de la Penya, and then climbs up the side of the barranc. After a punishing few minutes storming directly up the hill the path thankfully begins a rising traverse rightwards. After about 30mins the path arrives at what can only be described as a terrible disappointment. The slope we have been crossing proves not to be the main ridge and between it and the crest is the deep trench of **La Canal**. The path drops into the bed of the barranc where it passes a concrete font before climbing the other side.

Where it eventually emerges in a cultivated area the path turns left uphill. The track assaults the slope directly before relenting and angling across a scree slope to a purgatorially steep stone shoot and a final easy passage to the elusive ridge where Aitana leaps into view across the valley.

The path now follows the crest, crossing arêtes and minor tops before following a dirt road to **El Recingle** (1359m) with its crowning fire watching station from where the foresters have a superb 360 degree view.

Leave the summit by the marked path to the forestry road and turn left paralleling the line of the ridge. After 10mins at a junction turn left, still heading downhill. The road drops and then climbs quite steeply until it ends among trees. Carry on in the same line following a faint path through the wood and then out onto the open hillside, aiming for the summit of Pla de la Casa further along the ridge, on a faint track marked by the occasional cairn. The path drops steeply down into the col to an open field. Cross this to a cairn in the far left hand corner and from this take a faint path dropping down to a dirt road. Turn left along this and at a junction take the left hand branch still heading in the general direction of Pla de la Casa. Finally, with three quarters of the walk behind us, we reach the first genuine signpost, although neither branch points where we want to go. So ignore it and carry on down the broad track pausing only to admire the windows in the rock face above the path. Then, just like buses, a second signpost appears. This is the **Font Roja** with a plethora of signs. We follow the PR-CV 23-24 to Quatretondeta.

The gleaming pinnacles of Los Agules de Frares

The path contours down the side a barranc through interesting pinnacles and rocks before crossing an area of scree and then entering pleasant pinewoods.

This final section, especially in evening light, has the glorious finale of the **Agulles** above the path. This is a group of limestone pinnacles draped across the slope and one of the great natural sights of these mountains. They are sometimes known as Los Frares (the brothers or friars) but, strictly speaking, that name only applies to two of the towers, which are said to resemble the cowled figures of Capuchin monks.

Finally the path emerges on a wider road by the **Font de l'Espinal**. This is the start of a network of dirt roads. At a junction take the left hand option, essentially always aiming for Quatretondeta visible in the valley below. Finally the tracks arrive at the valley road where we cross to enter **Quatretondeta** and turn right down the main street to the car.

ALCOI AND THE WEST

The long summit ridge of the Cabeco d'Or (Walk 47)

WALK 47

Cabeco d'Or

Start/finish	Large layby at Pla de la Gralla, near Busot
Distance	11km
Grade	Moderate/Strenuous
Time	5hrs
Terrain	Narrow mountain tracks, some steep ascents and a short scramble
Height gain	850m
Map	IGN Jijona/Xixona
Access	From the N332 at El Campello follow signs for Busot. Do not enter the village but stay on the main road and shortly after passing the village take a road on the right signed to the Coves del Canelobre show caves. Continue up the road to where a large lay-by has been created behind a metal barrier.
Parking	Official car park.
Note	Do not be misled by the information board in the car park that quotes a time of 3 to 4hrs for the circuit and a climb of 480m. This is for the PR-CV 2 circuit, which does not actually visit the summit. The extra effort involved will add at least an hour to the time and 250m to the climb.

The 'Golden Head' of the Cabeco d'Or requires no explanation once it has been seen in the glow of early evening. The 1210m rocky crown seems to radiate an internal light. Its isolated position above a vast plain and the fact that this is the first major mountain seen by those heading north from Alicante only adds to its attraction. The top appears to be a maze of golden limestone crags and towers but on closer acquaintance this proves to be an illusion with the summit sitting on a sharply defined ridge.

From the car park head off along the dirt road. At a junction by a house turn right up a steep concrete road and carry on for about 15mins walking below striking

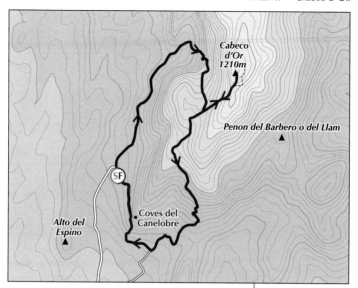

rockfaces to reach a ramshackle-looking house on a small col. Carry on down the road for a few more minutes to a junction and turn right uphill heading towards the crags.

After a few minutes the track reaches another small house, opposite which a path marked with yellow and white paint turns off to the right. Take this path which begins to climb in a series of zigzags before levelling out for a delightful wooded section to a col with a ruined house. The main PR-CV 2 carries straight on here but the summit path hooks back sharply leftwards. The first section is disarmingly level but the path soon rears up, climbing across the slope. When it reaches the cliffs it turns left along the very foot of the face, ascending gradually before climbing a short polished slab. The path them drops slightly to a gully with a natural rock pit and two wooden posts marked with yellow and white. Remember this; it is a crucial junction for the descent. For now, however, clamber up the short gully to emerge on the ridge. ▶

Here the views open out to the coast, northwards to the Penon de Ifach at Calp and inland to the distinctive shapes of the trinity of the Puig, the Ponoig and Xanchet.

199

The massif of the Cabeco d'Or

The track now follows the ridge leftwards to reach the summit of **Cabeco d'Or**, which is topped with a triangulation pillar and a metal box containing books of messages from those who have climbed it.

The **view** from the top is jaw-dropping in its scale and although the Cabeco is one of the outliers of the Costa Blanca there are fresh mountains in every direction. Spain is one of the most mountainous countries in Europe and this is a landscape where there is always another line of peaks beyond whatever summit you are on.

To descend reverse the track, taking care at the foot of the gully to climb up leftwards. Carrying on directly down the scree path is a temptation you would come to regret. Once back at the col with the ruined house pass in front of the building on a narrow path following yellow and white paint flashes dropping towards a notch between the main bulk of the mountain and a subsidiary ridge. This is the start of a long, meandering descent that will take up the next 45 to 60mins until the path passes beneath some power lines and reaches a sign for the PR-CV 226 pointing to the Coves del Canelobre. Follow this rightwards. When the path reaches some houses turn left down to a tarmac road and car park and a few metres beyond the houses take a track on the right signed PR-CV 2 Coves del Canelobre.

At the end of the track a footpath climbs the slope to the right, aiming for a col. The climb feels steep so late in proceedings but does slightly redeem itself by arriving at the café of the **Coves del Canelobre**. From here it is a gentle 10min stroll down the road to the car park.

WALK 48

Penya Migjorn

Start/finish	Xixona/Jijona
Distance	12km
Grade	Moderate
Time	3 to 4hrs
Terrain	Good paths, one exposed section
Height gain	750m
Map	847 Xixona/Jijona
Access	Xixona is easily reached from the A7 Alicante-Alcoi road. Go into the town centre and follow the signs for Tibi on the CV 810. The road climbs through the town and at a roundabout go right still following the CV 810. Just before the 2km marker turn right onto a narrow road marked by a bright yellow vertical pipe and signed 'Solo Residentes'. Park neatly here.

The 1226m Penya Migjorn and its neighbour, the much more impressive Penya del Mediodia, dominate Xixona. This walk follows the excellent PR-CV 212 throughout. The PR-CV network is a bit of mixed bag but this one is among the best and the waymarking and signposting exemplary so navigation is seldom a serious issue. It is, however, worth ignoring the timings posted on the signposts. They have either been measured by a particularly fleet-footed fell runner or else worked out by an especially inaccurate formula by someone who has never done the route. The walk might just as easily be called the circuit of the Mediodia as the route neatly circles this spectacular hill. The first half is characterised by the huge cliffs of the Mediodia and the second by a delightfully gentle valley.

Small wonder someone has gouged the word mentira (lie) into it to a clearly heartfelt depth.

From the junction by the yellow pipe walk up the narrow road for a hundred metres or so to a junction with a PR-CV 212 sign claiming the Penya Migjorn to be a mere 1hr and 10mins away. Do not believe it. Follow the road past two houses and after the second, where the tarmac runs out, continue uphill on the stony road marked by yellow and white paint flashes. On a right hand bend take a path on the left, marked with another PR-CV sign, which this time promises the Migjorn to be only an hour away. ◀

The looming rock face of the Mediodia

After another few minutes you reach a junction. Take the left hand fork aiming for a high col. When the path reaches a wider track, turn left and almost immediately curl behind a small house named **Pinyolapineta**.

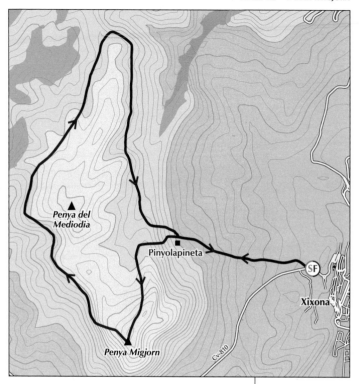

Continue up the broad track and within a couple of minutes look out for a narrow track on the right this time signed by yellow and white paint flashes and a cairn.

The path climbs steadily through trees, always heading for the col and after a final steep pull through the pines it emerges on the lip of a deep-cut ravine heading away southwards. To the right the triple buttresses of the Mediodia fall away into the valley. With your allotted hour and ten minutes from the first sign probably now long expired you may be wondering what has become of the Migjorn. To reach it you must climb leftwards still following the now-plentiful yellow and white flashes. The path traverses round the head of the gorge and climbing rock steps where the hands occasionally come into play. The going, while sometimes airy, is never particularly difficult.

At the next col it is worth taking the short detour rightwards to the summit of the Mediodia. Although purists may dismiss it as merely a subsidiary top of the Migjorn it is a splendid little summit that more than repays the few minutes it costs.

From the col climb leftwards to the summit of **Penya Migjorn**. The path leads easily upwards, passing a sign which promises the summit in 10mins. Yet again it is wrong, but just to keep you on your toes this time, it is gross overestimate. The concrete trig post is only a minute or so away. ◄

The view from the top is superb and well worth savouring.

From the summit return to the sign and take the left hand track marked to the Cova Els Corrals. The slope proves a natural stone staircase and in less than 20mins comes to a crossroads of paths, with not two but three of them marked PR-CV 212. Take the right hand option promising Xixona 1hr 20 mins. Hmmm.

This next section with its easy path shows the Mediodia to be yet another of those two-faced Costa Blanca mountains. The ascent was dominated by the huge overhanging rock wall while this side is all sweetness, green slopes and gentle slabs.

The track passes Cova Els Corrals, a ruined hut, where a sign points the way down the barranc still on the PR-CV 212. The path follows the valley until it meets the descending ridge where a signpost points rightwards down the slope. After a few minutes it curls back round the ridge on a narrow, stony track, which steepens and then crosses a dirt road leading to a smallholding before dropping to another dirt road. Turn right along this with the bulging face of the Mediodia once more looming above. At a junction with another road turn right to climb up over a rise to Pinyolapineta, having completed the full circuit of the mountain. Retrace your steps a few metres back down the road and then reverse the ascent path back down to **Xixona**.

Xixona is the centre for the manufacture of **Turon**, a kind of nougat, which is traditionally eaten around

Christmas throughout Spain. The town takes its
manufacture so seriously that it boasts a special
Turon Museum dedicated to its history.

WALK 49
Barranc del Cint

Start/finish	Alcoi/Alcoy
Distance	10km
Grade	Moderate
Time	3hrs
Terrain	Good paths and tracks
Height gain	600m
Map	Serra de Mariola (El Tossal)
Access	The barranc starts from the CV 796 road about 1km to the east of the former sanatorium, the Preventori. Given Alcoi's bewildering one way system the easiest approach is to take the CV 795 out of town, heading west signed to Banyeres de Mariola and then turn left onto the CV 796 signed to the Preventori. The entrance to the barranc is marked by an information board and the tall chimney of the old brickworks.
Parking	Entrance to barranc, or a little way further down the hill.
Note	Although this route is described as a circuit (for those who balk at the idea of covering the same ground twice), there is no denying that all the best terrain is to be found in the first half, and an out-and-back trip through the barranc to the ridge, which will take roughly 1hr 30mins to 2hrs, does avoid a rather complex finale.

Most mountain walks begin quietly as they leave the valley and build to
a crescendo as they gain height. The Barranc del Cint is rather different. It
begins with a dramatic flourish and undoubtedly the overture is the star of
this particular show. Even before you leave the tarmac the great yawning
entrance to the ravine, flanked by overhanging walls, is unmissable and after
you step into its jaws the views just keep getting better.

The route is marked with an abundance of red and white paint flashes for the long distance GR7 as well as yellow and white flashes from the PR, all of which are utterly superfluous as the path goes along a stone causeway along the narrow bed of the barranc from which even Spiderman would struggle to escape.

The causeway leads below the rock walls before climbing a flight of steps to an information board at the Ombria de Garrofer, where the path forks. Go directly ahead on the right hand option, which continues deeper into the **Barranc del Cint** before crossing the bed and then climbing steeply to pass a pumping station and reach a metalled road. Go up this for about 15mins to the hamlet of **Les Casetes de Vilaplana**.

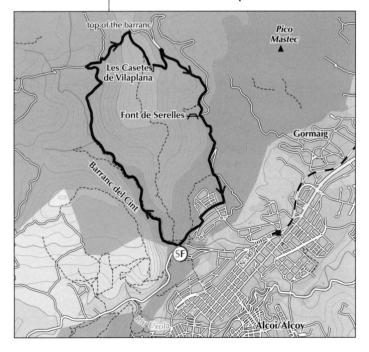

Entering the great chasm of the Barranc del Cint

Climbing the road the entire character of the walk changes. After being enclosed in the high walls of the barranc you are now in a huge open bowl with extensive views and wooded slopes out to the left and farmed terraces to the right. ▶

Just as you reach the houses on a left hand bend turn right along an unmade road opposite the corner of a house marked with red and white flashes. Where the track becomes concreted on a left hand bend take a narrow path climbing to the right.

Although this is unmarked it is part of the GR7 and has been much improved with the construction of wooden steps on the steepest sections and edging stone to delineate the route. Eventually the red paint marks do re-appear after a few hundred metres. ▶ Eventually the path arrives at a col where the views open out to the south with the ridges of the Serrella and Aitana ahead and the squat square keep of Cocentaina Castle out to the left below the slopes of Montcabrer.

When it reaches a four way junction of tracks turn right up the slight slope of the Mola Alta de Serelles. The

This whole area is also patrolled by Griffon Vultures, which can often be seen wheeling high above, their huge wings spread to catch the thermals.

The area has been badly affected by fire in recent years and, although now recovering, charred trees highlight the need for great care in this parched landscape.

junction is the place to turn back if opting to walk the barranc is both directions. Cross the top of the slope and begin to drop down, passing a distinctive semi-detached triangular crag and a nature reserve sign, taking hairpins below a ruined house. Ignore the broad track turning off directly below the house and instead carry on for another 100 metres to where a narrow footpath marked by a multitude of small cairns cuts back rightwards aiming for a clump of trees. The path goes through them and then steeply downhill until just before it reaches another dirt road a footpath breaks off rightwards, contouring across the hillside. Follow this across the slope to eventually arrive at the **Font de Serelles** picnic site, complete with tables, barbeque facilities and a brightly painted plunge pool.

Follow the access road downhill for about 10mins until just as it becomes concreted on a left hand hairpin an unmarked path breaks off directly ahead, initially contouring across the slope before diving downhill. At a junction of paths take the left hand, downhill, option to rejoin the road and a few metres later look out for a track again breaking off to the right, this time marked with green and white flashes.

Throughout the descent Alcoi has been an increasingly prominent feature of the view and now the track drops down to the ghostly road network of a partly built but apparently abandoned housing estate. The intention now is to work your way rightwards back towards the entrance to the barranc and the now-visible brickworks chimney while losing as little height as possible.

Turn right along the upper road of the estate to a T-junction and then turn left and immediately right again. At the end, by some occupied houses, drop leftwards to pass behind an electricity substation and take a dirt path across the barranc to reach the picnic area of the Font del Xorrador. From here a flight of wooden steps lead down and then a narrow ginnel slips between the houses to reach the road. Turn left and work your way uphill between houses passing a large electricity station to reach the road coming up from **Alcoi** and turn uphill to the car park.

WALK 50

Montcabrer

Start/finish	Cocentaina
Distance	18km
Grade	Strenuous
Time	6 to 7hrs
Terrain	Forest tracks, mountain paths
Height gain	1150m
Map	Serra de Mariola (El Tossal)
Access	Cocentaina is reached from the coast either by a scenic drive via Guadalest and Confrides or, more swiftly, by motorway from Alicante to the Cocentaina exit after Alcoi. The road from Confrides comes under the same junction. Drive into the town and at the third roundabout, 3km from the motorway junction and crowned by a large abstract sculpture of rusted metal, turn right following signs for Sant Cristofal. Follow the road uphill until it ends at a car park.

Cocentaina is about at the limit of what can realistically be reached in a day from the main coastal resorts although it is more accessible for those staying inland. Moreover, Montcabrer, at 1390m, the highest peak in the Mariola, is a Big Hill in anyone's book yet this walk through some of the region's most traditional scenery makes it well worth the effort. However, it may be as well to consider it a meandering circuit of this sprawling massif with the summit thrown in as a bonus rather than a direct assault.

Evening sunlight on the restored keep of Cocentaina

Leave the car park by the entrance and immediately turn right up a steep concrete road signed to the castle. Follow the road all the way to the top where it ends just below the squat keep. Where the road runs out take the middle of three paths and follow it up the crest of the ridge, encouraged by yellow and white paint marks. When the path reaches a road turn right and follow it for a few minutes downhill past several houses. Where the road begins to descend more steeply and just beyond the drive of a house look out for a path on the right marked by a cairn and yellow and white paint marks. Take this and after another couple of minutes, immediately after another house, look

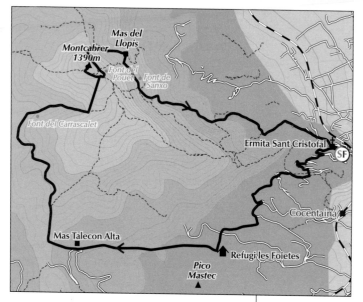

out for a narrower track on the right, again marked with paint, which leads through shaded pines traversing first of all below broken rocks and then more continuous crags before dropping to a dirt road. Here turn right following a sign for the PR-CV 37 **Refugi les Foietes**, 10mins away. By two metal posts at the entrance to a car park the path bears rightwards to skirt the parking area and then crosses a metalled road to enter the drive of the refuge. Just before reaching the buildings a PR-CV 37 sign to Coll de Sabata directs you rightwards down a rough road.

The road carries on through a delightfully traditional Spanish landscape of olive and almond groves set amid wooded hillsides dotted with fincas which look as though they could have sprung from the land themselves, a welcome change from the incongruous urbanizations nearer the coast.

Where the track comes to a fork ignore both roads and instead take a narrow path heading rightwards signed to the Coll. This becomes a track that contours gently round the mountain, coming to a huge area that has been devastated by fire. Carry on until the road starts to descend. There on a sharp right hand bend take a narrow path climbing away directly ahead from the apex of the bend.

It climbs steeply through the trees before crossing a barranc to enter another large area that has been ravaged by fire. Cross this and pass the substantial ruins of the **Mas Talecon Alta** and climb the short final slope to the Coll where the path turns rightwards uphill. As the path climbs the yellow and white flashes are joined by the red and white of the GR7 long-distance route. After a few minutes the track comes to a fork with the GR7 pointing to Montcabrer while the PR-CV 37 breaks away left to the Font de Julia. Both paths eventually reach the summit so we take the PR-CV 37.

The path contours round the mountain, undulating past the Font de Julia and at one stage drops deeply into a barranc before contouring round into another, the Barranc del Carrascalet, where a sign points uphill through the scrub oak towards the summit. On the way up the path passes the **Font del Carrascalet** at an altitude of 1100m. The path emerges on a broad col and rejoins the GR7, which has come over a subsidiary top. ◀

It is a short climb to the summit of **Montcabrer** before returning to the col and following the paint marks over the edge of the eastern flank. The path curls back leftwards beneath the summit rocks. The path initially seems to be heading in the wrong direction but carry on following the paint marks past the **Font del Pouet** a long way rightwards, mainly marked by the white and red of the GR7. After it passes a small shrine in the shape of a tiny stone house look out a minute or so later for a signpost pointing rightwards for the PR-CV 37 to **Mas del Llopis** and **Font de Sanxo**. Take this. When it reaches a cross path turn left again making for the ruins on the promontory ahead and the distant tower of the castle. At the ruins take the higher path to pass the Font del Mas de Sanxo where it turns abruptly downhill to begin a steep

The summit rocks of Montcabrer stand out to the left while to the east the view opens up to the mountains of the coast and the reservoir of Beniarres, a mocking sight on a hot day.

Deluxe butty stop on the descent of Montcabrer

and rapid descent. This involves clambering down some rocky steps but as it drops the more exposed sections are provided with a wooden rail. Once the picnic tables and pergola arrive it seems civilisation cannot be far away, but in fact it is at least another 30mins the **Ermita Sant Cristofal** and to the car park.

Along the way is a viewpoint with a tiled orientation panel naming the surrounding tops and towns. When the path joins a road by a tiled information sign turn right to follow it downhill. When it forks, take the right hand option and pass behind the buildings to reach the car park.

213

APPENDIX A
Route summary table

Walk	Start/Finish	Distance	Height gain	Grade	Time	Page
The North						
1	Plana de Justa, near Xabia	15km	800m	Strenuous	6hrs	29
2	Pego	11km	773m	Moderate	4hrs	31
3	Benimeli	6km	350m	Moderate	3hrs	35
4	Pedreguer	12km	550m	Moderate	3hrs, 30mins	39
5	Font d'Aixa	10km	490m	Moderate	3hrs, 30mins–4hrs	43
6	Gata de Gorgos	12km	470m	Moderate	3–4hrs	46
7	Cumbre del Sol	8km	350m	Easy/ Moderate	3–4hrs	50
Inland from Calp						
8	Calp	3km	332m	Moderate	2hrs	54
9	Calp	9km	440m	Moderate	3hrs	56
10	Casas de Runar or Casas de Bernia	14km	480m	Strenuous	4–5hrs	60
11	Near Pinos	9km	670m	Scramble	5hrs	64
12	Casas de Bernia	8km	510m	Moderate/ Scramble	5hrs	68
13	El Masserof	6km	400m	Moderate	4hrs	72
14	El Masserof	8km	400m	Scramble	4hrs	75
15	Near Xalo	13km	525m	Moderate	3–4hrs	79
16	Xalo	12km	410m	Moderate	3–4hrs	83
17	Parcent	15km	825m	Moderate/ Strenuous	5–6hrs	86
18	Xalo	12km	585m	Moderate	4hrs 30mins–5hrs	90

Walk	Start/Finish	Distance	Height gain	Grade	Time	Page
19	Murla	5.5km	500m	Moderate	4hrs	95
20	Fleix	12km	420m	Moderate	3–4hrs	98
21	Collado de Garga or 3km further on	6km	275m	Easy/ Moderate	2–3hrs	102
22	Benimaurell	16km	900m	Strenuous	4–5hrs	106
23	Fleix	12km	350m	Moderate	3–4hrs	110
24	Benigembla	14km	730m	Strenuous	5hrs	114
25	Near Benigembla or near Pla de Petracos	20km or 9km	640m or 80m	Strenuous or Moderate	5–6hrs or 3hrs	119
26	Alcala de la Jovada	9km	290m	Moderate	3hrs	124
Inland from Benidorm						
27	Benidorm/Albir	10km	1000m	Strenuous	3–4hrs	128
28	Near Callosa d'En Sarria	11km	470m	Moderate	3hrs 30mins–4hrs	131
29	Bolulla	8km	520m	Moderate	3–4hrs	134
30	Bolulla/Raco Roig	8km	250m	Moderate	3hrs	138
31	Between Tarbena and Castell de Castells	17km	525m	Moderate	5hrs	141
32	Between Tarbena and Castell de Castells	7.5km	200m	Easy	2–2hrs 30mins	145
33	Guadalest Rservoir	10km	Negligible	Easy	3hrs	148
34	Near Benifato	10km	550m	Moderate	4hrs	151
35	Near Guadalest	11km	575m	Moderate	3–4hrs	155
36	Above Sella	6km	250m	Easy	2hrs	158

Walk	Start/Finish	Distance	Height gain	Grade	Time	Page
37	Near Sella	12km	320m	Moderate	3–4hrs	160
38	Vall de Guadar	14km	620m	Moderate	4hrs	164
39	Near Finestrat	12km	640m	Moderate	4–5hrs	167
40	Finestrat	11km	600m	Moderate	3–4hrs	173
41	Els Amanellos	10km	590m	Moderate	3hrs	176
42	Coll del Pouet	4.6km (plus approach)	625m	Strenuous	2hrs 30mins–3hrs (plus approach)	178
The Serrella						
43	Castell de Castells	11.5k	430m	Moderate	3–4hrs	182
44	Famorca	12km	730m	Moderate	4–5hrs	185
45	Fageca	13km	690m	Strenuous	4–5hrs	189
46	Quatretondeta	13km	750m	Strenuous	5–6hrs	193
Alcoi and the West						
47	Near Busot	11km	850m	Moderate/ Strenuous	5hrs	198
48	Xixona	12km	750m	Moderate	3–4hrs	201
49	Alcoi	10km	600m	Moderate	3hrs	205
50	Cocentaina	18km	1150m	Strenuous	6–7hrs	209

APPENDIX B

Valenciano–Spanish–English glossary

Valenciano	Spanish	English
abaix	abajo	below
aljub	aljibe	well, cistern
alt	alto	height, hill
area recreativa	area recreativa	picnic area
avenc	simas	potholes, fissures
baix	bajo	low
bancal	bancal	terrace
barranc	barranco	gorge, ravine
cami	camino	track, country road
casa	casa	house
caseta	casita	small house, hut
castell	castillo	castle, fort
caca	caza	hunting
coll/collado/collau	collado	pass
coto de caca	coto de caza	hunting ground
cova	cueva	cave
cruz	cruz	cross
cumbre, cim	cim	summit
disposit d'aigua	deposito de agua	water tank
embassament	embalse	reservoir
era	era	threshing floor
ermita	ermita	hermitage, chapel
finca	finca	country house, farm
font	fuente	well, spring
forat	hoyo	hole

Valenciano	Spanish	English
horta	huerta	market garden
llac	lago	lake
llavador	laverdero	wash house
lloma	loma	shoulder of a hill
mas	mas	farmhouse
mig, mij	medio	middle
mirador	mirador	viewpoint
moli	molino	mill
muntanya	montana	mountain
nevera	nevera	snowpit
particular	particular	private
paso	pass	pass
penya	pena	cliff, rocky peak
platja	playa	beach
port	puerto	pass
pou/pouet	pozo	well
pont	puente	bridge
presa	presa	dam
privado	privado	private
puig	cerro, collina	hill
refugi	refugio	climbers' refuge
riu	rio	river
roca	roca	rock
sender	sendero	path
serra	sierra	ridge, mountain range
torre	torre	tower
vall	valle	valley

APPENDIX C
Useful contacts

Tourism on the Costa Blanca is so well developed that there is a wealth of information on the internet regarding flights and accommodation.

Walking

Tourist offices
Information is frustratingly fragmented as local tourism offices, often at town halls, usually cover their own district only with little or no wider view. Pego (www. pegoilesvalls.es) and Moraira/Teulada Edificio Espai La Senieta, Av de Madrid 15, 03725, Teulada, Moraira, I found the most useful. Benidorm the least. Calp was also helpful (www.calpe.es). Wider information is available from the Alicante tourist office site (www.costablanca.org).

Costa Blanca Walkers (www. cbmwalkers.org) is a mainly British walking group. The website lists a programme of weekly walks as well as advice and links to routes. Costa Blanca Mountain Friends (www.costablancamountainfriends.com) contains more useful information on Spanish walking in general.

Maps
Useful maps are listed in 'Maps and language'. These are available locally from Libreria Europa (C Oscar Espla 2, 03710, Calp, Tel 96 583 5824, www.libreria-europa-calpe.com). Good English is spoken and there is a swift online service. Some can also be ordered in advance from UK suppliers such as Stanfords (12–14 Long Acre, London, WC2E 9BR, Tel 0207 8361321, www.stanfords. co.uk) and The Map Shop (15 High Street, Upton-upon-Severn, WR8 0HJ, Tel 01684 593146, www.themapshop.co.uk).

Insurance
Normal holiday insurance may not cover some walks and scrambles. If in doubt specialist insurance is available from British Mountaineering Council, 177–179, Burton Road, West Didsbury, Manchester, M20 2BB, Tel 0161 4456111 (www.thebmc. co.uk).

Insurance can also be arranged through non-British mountaineering organisations, notably the Austrian Alpine Club (www.aacuk.org.uk) but check it covers your needs. Some commercial insurers will also cover mountaineering but again be careful to check you have the appropriate cover.

Public transport
The major bus operator in the area is Llorente Bus Company which runs almost 50 routes around the Benidorm/Alicante region. However these are mainly between the coastal towns, and services into the interior are patchy and infrequent making them of little use for walkers who will find a hire car much more convenient. Each journey on a Llorente Bus has a fixed price and tickets are purchased on board. Frequent travellers have the option to buy a book of 20 tickets at a reduced rate per ticket on the price of individually bought tickets. More information on http://costablanca. angloinfo.com/information/transport/ public-transport/regional-bus-services/ or from Llorente Bus, Calle Castello, 10, Poligono Industrial Finestrat, 03509 Alicante, Tel 965 854322. Within towns the buses are usually locally operated.

LISTING OF CICERONE GUIDES

Via Ferratas of the French Alps
Walking in Corsica
Walking in Provence – East
Walking in Provence – West
Walking in the Auvergne
Walking in the Cevennes
Walking in the Dordogne
Walking in the Haute Savoie – North & South
Walking in the Tarentaise and Beaufortain Alps
Walks in the Cathar Region

GERMANY

Germany's Romantic Road
Hiking and Biking in the Black Forest
Walking in the Bavarian Alps

HIMALAYA

Annapurna
Bhutan
Everest
Garhwal and Kumaon
Langtang with Gosainkund and Helambu
Manaslu
The Mount Kailash Trek
Trekking in Ladakh
Trekking in the Himalaya

ICELAND & GREENLAND

Trekking in Greenland
Walking and Trekking in Iceland

IRELAND

The Irish Coast to Coast Walk
The Mountains of Ireland

ITALY

Gran Paradiso
Sibillini National Park
Shorter Walks in the Dolomites
The Way of St Francis
Through the Italian Alps
Trekking in the Apennines
Trekking in the Dolomites
Via Ferratas of the Italian Dolomites: Vols 1 & 2
Walking in Abruzzo
Walking in Italy's Stelvio National Park
Walking in Sardinia
Walking in Sicily
Walking in the Central Italian Alps

Walking in the Dolomites
Walking in Tuscany
Walking in Umbria
Walking on the Amalfi Coast
Walking the Italian Lakes

MEDITERRANEAN

Jordan – Walks, Treks, Caves, Climbs and Canyons
The Ala Dag
The High Mountains of Crete
The Mountains of Greece
Treks and Climbs in Wadi Rum
Walking and Trekking on Corfu
Walking in Malta
Western Crete

NORTH AMERICA

British Columbia
The Grand Canyon
The John Muir Trail
The Pacific Crest Trail

SOUTH AMERICA

Aconcagua and the Southern Andes
Hiking and Biking Peru's Inca Trails
Torres del Paine

SCANDINAVIA

Walking in Norway

SLOVENIA, CROATIA AND MONTENEGRO

The Islands of Croatia
The Julian Alps of Slovenia
The Mountains of Montenegro
Trekking in Slovenia
Walking in Croatia
Walking in Slovenia: The Karavanke

SPAIN AND PORTUGAL

Mountain Walking in Southern Catalunya
Spain's Sendero Histórico: The GR1
The Mountains of Nerja
The Northern Caminos
Trekking through Mallorca
Walking in Madeira
Walking in Mallorca
Walking in Menorca
Walking in the Algarve

Walking in the Cordillera Cantabrica
Walking in the Sierra Nevada
Walking on Gran Canaria
Walking on La Gomera and El Hierro
Walking on La Palma
Walking on Lanzarote and Fuerteventura
Walking on Tenerife
Walking the GR7 in Andalucia
Walks and Climbs in the Picos de Europa

SWITZERLAND

Alpine Pass Route
Central Switzerland
The Swiss Alps
Tour of the Jungfrau Region
Walking in the Bernese Oberland
Walking in the Valais
Walking in Ticino
Walks in the Engadine

TECHNIQUES

Geocaching in the UK
Indoor Climbing
Lightweight Camping
Map and Compass
Mountain Weather
Outdoor Photography
Polar Exploration
Rock Climbing
Sport Climbing
The Hillwalker's Manual

MINI GUIDES

Alpine Flowers
Avalanche!
Navigating with a GPS
Navigation
Pocket First Aid and Wilderness Medicine
Snow

MOUNTAIN LITERATURE

8000 metres
A Walk in the Clouds
Abode of the Gods
Unjustifiable Risk?

For full information on all our guides, books and eBooks, visit our website:
www.cicerone.co.uk.

Walking – Trekking – Mountaineering – Climbing – Cycling

Over 40 years, Cicerone have built up an outstanding collection of over 300 guides, inspiring all sorts of amazing adventures.

Every guide comes from extensive exploration and research by our expert authors, all with a passion for their subjects. They are frequently praised, endorsed and used by clubs, instructors and outdoor organisations.

All our titles can now be bought as **e-books**, **ePubs** and **Kindle** files and we also have an online magazine – **Cicerone Extra** – with features to help cyclists, climbers, walkers and trekkers choose their next adventure, at home or abroad.

Our website shows any **new information** we've had in since a book was published. Please do let us know if you find anything has changed, so that we can publish the latest details. On our **website** you'll also find great ideas and lots of detailed information about what's inside every guide and you can buy **individual routes** from many of them online.

It's easy to keep in touch with what's going on at Cicerone by getting our monthly **free e-newsletter**, which is full of offers, competitions, up-to-date information and topical articles. You can subscribe on our home page and also follow us on **Facebook** and **Twitter** or dip into our **blog**.

Cicerone – the very best guides for exploring the world.

CICERONE

2 Police Square Milnthorpe Cumbria LA7 7PY
Tel: 015395 62069 info@cicerone.co.uk
www.cicerone.co.uk and **www.cicerone-extra.com**